Applied linguistics for English-Spanish translation

ANA FERNÁNDEZ GUERRA

Bibliographic information published by the Deutsche Nationalbibliothek

The Deutsche Nationalbibliothek lists this publication in the Deutsche
Nationalbibliografie; detailed bibliographic data are available
in the Internet at http://dnb.d-nb.de .

ISBN 978-3-8325-3778-4

Logos Verlag Berlin GmbH
Comeniushof, Gubener Str. 47,
10243 Berlin
Tel.: +49 (0)30 42 85 10 90
Fax: +49 (0)30 42 85 10 92
INTERNET: http://www.logos-verlag.de

The aim of the present book is to give an overview of (and an insight into) translation, as well as an introduction to some of the major linguistic theories used to explain the task of translating, and to the main problems involved in English-Spanish translation.

Contents will briefly focus on the concept of translation, the main approaches applied to the theory and practice of translation, how linguistic paradigms have contributed to translation studies, the role of the translator and translation competence, the main theoretical problems and controversial issues (translatability vs. untranslatability, fidelity vs. fluency, equivalence vs. adequacy, etc.), translation strategies and techniques, practical problems in English-Spanish translation, translation and new technologies, and the evaluation of translation.

Each chapter includes three theoretical sections dealing with the abovementioned issues, as well as a forth section with suggestions for further readings, and a final fifth section with translation tasks and questions, since theory and practice are both equally important and interdependent. With these contents in mind, students, language learners, teachers or researchers following the present book, are expected to:

- Identify translation as an interdiscipline and the main approaches to translation studies.
- Identify the main contribution of the linguistic paradigms to the theory and practice of translation.
- Know the skills required of the translator and the importance of acquiring translation competence.
- Explain the main theoretical problems and controversial issues hat nowadays seem to affect the theory and practice of translation.
- Apply their knowledge of translation techniques and strategies to solve the problems involved in English-Spanish translation.
- Discuss their findings or difficulties in English-Spanish translation.
- Use new technologies that can be useful when translating.
- Compare, analyse and evaluate different translations.

Ana Fernández Guerra
Universitat Jaume I, Spain

Contents

Abbreviations

AS	Overall assessment
CAT/MAT	Machine or computer-aided translation
CONT	Changes in content
CULT	Cultural-bound words
FAHQT	Fully automatic high quality translation
GR	Morphosyntactic aspects
HAMT	Human-assisted machine translation
LEX	Lexico-semantic aspects
MAHT	Machine-assisted human translation
MT	Machine translation
PRAG	Pragmatic aspects
SC	Source culture
SL	Source language
STY	Writing style and register
TC	Target culture
TECH	Translation technique
TEXT	Textual cohesion and coherence
TIP	Spelling and punctuation aspects
TL	Target language

List of figures

1. Applied linguistics for translation: introduction

1.1. The concept of *translation*

The term *translation* is an incredibly wide concept, which can be understood in many different ways. Examining the origin of the term, we should point out that, etymologically, translation refers to "bringing across" or "carrying across", and originated from the Latin "translatio" (*trans* meaning "across" and *latum*, supine form of *fero*, "bring" or "carry"). Translation itself is an old issue: the renowned *Tower of Babel* is the Biblical explanation for the diversity of languages, meaning "gate to God" in Assyrian and "to confuse" in Hebrew.

In trying to understand what translation is, it seems wise, first of all, to take a look at definitions that can be found in dictionaries of language and linguistics. There are millions of studies dealing with the concept of translation (and with many other aspects related to the task of translating, of course). If we take the *Diccionario de la lengua española* (DRAE 2001) and the *Diccionario de uso español* (María Moliner 1998), for example, we will find that the verb *to interpret* and/or *translate* (often synonymous and interchangeable) are defined at three different levels:

- To interpret is to substitute one "code" for another; so as to explain something hidden, not clear or unknown.
- To translate is *to express something in another language* or to change/transfer a linguistic content (information) from one language into another.
- To interpret or translate is also *to infer the meaning of gestures, symbols,* and the like, used in a theatre play, in a piece of art, etc. which are the expression of a given "content" or message.

The noun *translation* or *interpretation* is understood as the act of translating/interpreting, as well as the result of such activity: "something that is or has been translated/interpreted". The DRAE adds various nuances as regards the correct *interpretation* of laws; and the *translation* as a correct interpretation of a written text.

The same interchangeability between translation and interpretation can be found in English dictionaries. The *Collins English Dictionary*, for example, defines *interpreter* as a person who translates orally from one language into another; a person who interprets the work of others (and also the part of a program that translates the code in which instructions are written into machine language for immediate use by the computer); and *translator* as a person or machine that translates speech or writing.

If we turn to specialised dictionaries (on philology and linguistics), which should be more specific in their definitions, we will find the following:

Lázaro Carreter's *Diccionario de términos filológicos* (1974) again treats translation as a synonym of interpretation; and defines both in terms of classical rhetoric, *interpretation* being one of the processes of *amplification* consisting in "saying with other words what has been just said".

According to Hartmann and Stork's *Dictionary of Language and Linguistics* (1976), *interpretation* is an oral translation from one language into another carried out by a person who knows both languages as well as the subject matter; and *translation* is the process or result of converting information from one language (or one variety of a language, like a dialect, or a technolect) into another language (or a variety of it). When translating material which is written or registered in natural languages, the aim consists both in reproducing, as close as possible, all the grammatical and lexical characteristics of the source language (SL) by finding appropriate equivalents in the target language (TL), or *equivalence* in "expression"; and in retaining, at the same time, all the factic information present in the original text, or *equivalence* in "content".

Translations are then classified according to the following aspects:

1. *The degree of equivalence reached* (taking into account both fluency and fidelity), thus distinguishing among:
   - Word-for-word translation: translating words with "fidelity" but without taking into account the final cohesion of the message (*without any "fluency"*);
   - Literal translation: in which a slight reformulation is made; is concerned therefore with fidelity but *reaching a "minimum of fluency"* in the TL; and
   - Free or idiomatic translation: in which the message of the source language is completely re-formulated in the TL, so as to express it freely (*with complete "fluency"*).

2. *The object of translation* (that is, what is going to be or has to be translated), making a clear distinction between:
   - Literary translation: of works of literature (poetry, drama, ...) in which emotions and stylistic features are important and in which Fluency is essential.

- Pragmatic translation: in which the importance lies in the factic information to be transmitted; and in which fidelity will, then, be the essential goal.

3. *The mode/channel in which translation* (transmission of information) is effected, thus differentiating among:
   - Translation (proper): transmission of human written material.
   - Interpretation: transmission of human oral (spoken) material.
   - Automatic translation: the type carried out with the help of a machine (a computer).

Other specialised dictionaries and encyclopaedic works add very little to what has been summarised in the previous paragraphs:

In Lewandowski's *Linguistisches Wörterbuch* (1982), *interpretation* is understood as the expression and explanation of contents in literary texts, as the coordination of meanings and symbols of an abstract system (formal language, ideal world), and as the semantic understanding of deep structures based on surface structures (along Chomsky's line of thinking). While *translation* is understood as the transfer of denotative and connotative information of a given text, using the linguistic resources of another language.

After acknowledging Hartmann and Stork's types of translation and making it clear that literal and word-for-word translations may be possible *only* when sentences are very simple or when we take into account *only* the factic content, disregarding structural and semantic correspondences (as in the case of *dos y dos son cuatro*, 'two plus two make four'; or *Pedro está en casa*, 'Peter is at home', etc.), Lewandowski concludes that, when translating, the *ideal* must be to account for the pragmatic and cultural connotations of the original text (to obtain total *fidelity*); and, when the language itself is an information carrier (as is the case in poetic and aesthetic texts), to take into account also the linguistic means in the TL that may carry the same structural and semantic correspondences present in the SL, to obtain total *fluency*.

In von Wilpert's encyclopaedic dictionary *Sachwörterbuch der Literatur* (1979) we find more or less the same understanding of both translation and interpretation: *Interpretation* is understood as the attempt to explain a written work of literature in terms of its *form*, its *content* and its *literary language* along the line of thought in modern poetics; whereas *translation* would be simply the transfer of written information from one language into another. Such a transfer can be made:

- From one modern language (English, French, ...) into another (Spanish, Italian, ...).
- From a dead language (Latin, for example) into a modern language.

- From a dialect into the generally accepted language in a community (for example, from *Plattdeutsch* into present-day German).
- From a previous stage of a language into another stage (from Old English into Present-day English, for instance).

He mentions that literature in translation has been useful, positive and fruitful in both favouring the exchange of culture and a revival of old cultural traditions, and contributing to the shaping of most vernacular literatures (like the influence of Homer's and Shakespeare's works in German literature). But we observe a good deal of pessimism when he concludes that literary translation, with the equivalence of *all æsthetic* and *euphonic values* (rhyme, rhythm, metre, melody, stylistic nuances, sensorial connotative elements, etc.) is *practically impossible* since we have to restrict ourselves to the possibilities of our own language; and therefore the translator has to limit him/herself to aiming at certain *aurea mediocritas* between "fidelity" and "freedom", between Scylla's servile translation and Charybdis's free ("re-creating") translation of an original literary text.

Finally, Roman Jakobson (1959) makes a very important distinction between three types of translation:

- Intralingual translation, within the same language, which involves rewording or paraphrasing. For example, in the case of the book "Harry Potter and the Philosopher's Stone" (Bloomsbury 1997) some intralingual changes were made when it appeared in the USA as "Harry Potter and the Sorcerer's Stone" (Scholastic 1998), changing some British words, such as *biscuits, football,* or *rounders,* with the American *cookies, soccer* and *baseball.*
- Interlingual translation, from one language into another (in his interpretation, only interlingual translation is deemed 'translation proper').
- Intersemiotic translation or transmutation, which involves the interpretation of a verbal sign by a non-verbal sign, for example image or music, no-smoking or exit sign in public places or icons and symbols on the computer screen, etc.

1.2. Translation as an academic discipline

The concept of *translation* should also be defined from a wider perspective, not only from the point of view of what translating entails, but also as a field of study and an academic discipline in its own right. In fact, the word 'translation' is used to denote a manual or theoretical work of the subject or, in other words, an academic area of study and reseach.

Actually, as an academic discipline, it is only about 50 years old, since translation was before mainly used, analysed and discussed for language teaching, with a secondary status in academia. Of course, we have many studies dealing with translation, going back to Cicero (106-43 B.C.), for instance, in which theories on literal and free translation started to be discussed. But translation, as an academic field of study, can be considered a quite young academic discipline, since it only began to emerge in the 1970s, and it is still considered by many scholars as an immature and emerging discipline. As Snell-Hornby (2006: 150) said, quoting Lefevere, translation studies as an academic discipline is still suffering from childhood diseases. Theories on translation, though, have been given diverse names over the history, as can be seen below:

- English: Translatology, science of translation, translation theory, etc.
- German: Translatologie, Übersetzungswissenschaft, Übersetzungstheorie, etc.
- French: traductologie, science de la traduction, théorie de la traduction, etc.
- Spanish: traductología, ciencia de la traducción, teoría de la traducción, etc.

James S. Holmes, as we will see in the next chapter, argued for the name "Translation Studies" as the standard term of the discipline concerned with the study of translation at large, including all theoretical frameworks, all types of translations, research on the field, pedagogical activities, etc.

Nowadays, we can say there is an increasing interest in the translation profession as such, and in the teaching of translation. As a matter of fact, more and more studies on the didactics of translation are published, and more and more degrees on Translation Studies are been offered lately. Malmkjær (2004: 2), for instance, indicates the importance of translation degrees:

> One means towards avoiding a split between a profession and its academic discipline is to ensure that teaching programmes have face validity for members of those professions in which students might seek employment. For a translation programme to achieve face validity for the translation profession, the profession needs to be convinced that graduates of the programme have acquired at least some of the knowledge and skills necessary for success in the profession.

1.3. Levels of linguistic analysis that are important

Translation is certainly a quite complex task, and not as easy as it sounds to be, since it cannot be considered as a mere mechanical process in which each word can be replaced by another word in the TL. Rather, there are many aspects that have to be taken into account when translating. In this section we will focus on the aspects of language that are important in translation (though there are, obviously, many other issues to take into account, such as culture, which, most of the times, has its representation or realisation on the language; along with many other issues, as we will see in the following chapters). As regards linguistic aspects that are important when translating, we should consider at least six interdependent components (or component sub-systems of the language, or levels of linguistic analysis). Their importance is clear due to the following facts: (1) knowledge of the language system itself (both SL and TL) is important; and (2) these levels have an effect on translation:

- PHONOLOGY: the study of the sound system and rules governing them. A knowledge of the sound system is necessary and it can affect translations (for example, in the case of palindromes, like *Alí tomó tila*; or alliterations, as in *Dales las lilas*, in which trying to transfer the same content and stylistic effect can be quite difficult).

- MORPHOLOGY: form and structure of words, patterns of inflection and derivation of words (for example the translation of *Are you tired?* as *Estás* or *Estáis* or *Está cansado*).

- SYNTAX: the principles of word order as well as of phrase and sentence construction (as in *blue car, coche azul* and not *azul coche*).

- LEXICON: the set of all morphemes and the vocabulary system (that can affect the translation of simple words, as *cook* for *cocinar* or *cocinero*, lexical relations like hyponyms, etc.).

- SEMANTICS: the study of meaning, changes in meaning, and the principles that govern the relationship between sentences or words and their meanings (*corner* for both *rincón* and *esquina*).

- PRAGMATICS: the study of those aspects of language that cannot be considered in isolation from its use or, in other words, the socio-cultural conventions for using the other components. This includes many features, like indirectness (*Where's my cake? The dog looks happy...*), politeness values (asking for a coke in Spanish could perfectly be *Una cola-cola*, but in an English pub we could probably say *Could I have a coke, please?*), cultural values (the expression *¡y un jamón!*, for instance), etc.

We certainly need to take into account all those language components when we translate a text, and it is not an easy task, since they are all interrelated, as can be seen in *Figure 1*.

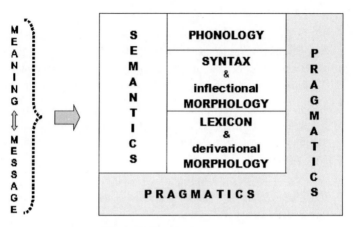

Figure 1: *Language components.*

1.4. Further readings

Fernández Guerra, A. 2001. *El arte de traducir y la máquina de traducir. Antagonismo o síntesis integradora.* Valencia: Albatros.
Ordudari, M. 2008. Good Translation: Art, Craft, or Science? *Translation Journal* 12/1. http://translationjournal.net/journal/43theory.htm

1.5. Tasks: getting started

1. Translate the following passages. You will encounter several difficulties in each one. When translating, think first of the meaning and of possible ambiguities. Which structural and idiomatic problems do these sentences present? Compare your translations with the group and discuss all the alternatives proposed.

  (1) J. Pérez de la Universidad de North Carolina escribe sobre literatura postfranquista y sus libros son muy conocidos. Me cuenta que su hermano, que es biólogo, viste siempre corbata y camisa de seda. Me pregunta también cómo hemos encontrado la dirección de Alba.

(2) "El fin de esta vida es el desarrollo de la personalidad ... Hoy los hombres se asustan de sí mismos". Tales palabras, dichas por un despreciable personaje de Oscar Wilde, transparentan algo que Wilde llevaba dentro de sí mismo. (F. Suárez).

(3) Muy señores míos:

Tengo que informarles que hemos estudiado su solicitud de cotización por supervisión de descarga de *concentración de cobre* en el muelle El Durazno, de Santiago de Chile, y que nuestra tarifa es de UF 0,012 (cero coma cero doce Unidades de Fomento) por tonelada métrica, IVA incluido.

(4) The Law says that every person who was imprisoned on the 4-1-1995 shall be released on bail. It also says that no tradesman, workman, labourer or any other person whatsoever shall be allowed to work in the vicinity of an airfield on Sundays.

(5) The man at the door is Tom Hill, whose shop is called "The Price is Right". It is closed every day at 5 pm. He also has a car showroom with a notice saying "Guaranteed Used Cars".

(6) Dr Watson returns to Baker Street to find Sherlock Holmes painting the door of their house a bright yellow colour. "What's that, Holmes?" asks Watson. "Lemon entry, my dear Watson", he replies.

(7) "You should be on Mastermind", said Vic to his girlfriend. Vic was tiring rapidly of TV dinners and Asian restaurants, which was all that Rummidge seemed to offer the single man.

(8) The Llanabba Silver Band was third at the North Wales Eisteddfod last month. The conductor sounds not unlike David Frost.

(9) "O brave new world", said Robyn, who had spent the morning at Harrods buying with her eyes, "where only the managing directors have jobs. But if they let you go, isn't there something called a golden handshake?"

(10) "As regards the Fiesta, I didn't forget to put a card in the Co-op last week", said Tim, as he walked out of his front door, solid and sure of himself, in a little side street full of suburban gardens and comfortable houses.

2. How do *you* feel about translation?

(a) Translation will always be 'the boring bit' of a language course.

❏ Yes   ❏ No   ❏ I don't know

(b) Translation is not as important as knowing the language.

❐ Yes ❐ No ❐ I don't know

(c) Knowing translation theories and approaches does not mean you can translate better.

❐ Yes ❐ No ❐ I don't know

(d) Translation is a skill that demands an apprenticeship.

❐ Yes ❐ No ❐ I don't know

(e) Translation helps to contrast the students' native language with the target language.

❐ Yes ❐ No ❐ I don't know

(f) A good knowledge of the language systems is very important because all levels of linguistic analysis have an effect on translation.

❐ Yes ❐ No ❐ I don't know

(g) In translating, the ideal must be to account for total fidelity and total fluency.

❐ Yes ❐ No ❐ I don't know

(h) Translating refers to the intellectual process by which a message is transferred into another language.

❐ Yes ❐ No ❐ I don't know

(i) Learning how to translate is learning how to think in order to communicate accurately the ideas of another person.

❐ Yes ❐ No ❐ I don't know

(j) As a process of interpretation and communication, translating transcends language.

❐ Yes ❐ No ❐ I don't know

3. What is translation? What aspects of language are important in translation?

4. Understanding and re-expressing: Each of these sentences can be rewritten more briefly, changing the linguistic expression, but without changing the meaning (taken from Mott 2011: 71). Rewrite them in as few words as possible. Then translate them and compare your translations (and their length) with someone else's:

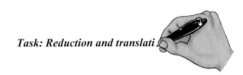

Task: Reduction and translati

(a) It is not uncommon to encounter sentences which, though they contain a great number of words and are constructed in a highly complex way, none the less turn out on inspection to convey very little meaning of any kind.

(b) In her employment, Janice manifested a thoroughly satisfactory degree of energy and efficiency.

(c) Many young ladies in their teens manifest a distinct tendency to prefer the company of members of the opposite sex who are no longer in the first flower of youth.

(d) It is undeniable that the vast majority of non-native learners of the English language experience considerable difficulty in mastering the phonetic patterns of the language.

(e) I have been obliged to abandon the belief which I previously held in the existence of a benevolent, white-haired, bearded figure who was accustomed to visiting private houses on the anniversary of the birth of the founder of the Christian faith in order to distribute gifts to the very young.

(f) Tea, whether of the China or Indian variety, is well known to be high on the list of those beverages which are most frequently drunk by the inhabitants of the British Isles.

(g) One of the most noticeable phenomena in any big city, such as London or Paris, is the steadily increasing number of petrol-driven vehicles, some in private ownership, others belonging to the public transport system, which congest the roads and render rapid movement from one place to another more difficult year by year.

(h) "The main problem with which I am faced is to decide whether it is preferable to continue in existence, or whether it would, on balance, be a more advisable policy to abandon the struggle".

2. Linguistic paradigms and approaches applied to the theory and practice of translation

2.1. Interdisciplinarity in Translation Studies

Translation is nowadays considered a field of study in its own right. However, its place within linguistic studies, as well as its relation to other disciplines, is still a matter of debate, and many approaches and theories towards its study vary depending on the scholars' perspectives. Amongst translation specialists, we can find three main perspectives as regards where to place translation studies:

On the one hand, many scholars see translation as a branch of the interdisciplinary field of Applied Linguistics, which investigates and provides solutions to language-related real-life problems, and translation goes together with studies related to multilingualism, contrastive linguistics, second language acquisition, and many other branches. Catford (1965: 20) is perhaps one of the most renowned and pioneering authors showing this point of view: "[...] Clearly, then, any theory of translation must draw upon a theory of language — a general linguistic theory".

Since the 1980s, however, some theorists started to claim that language is only the raw material of translation (Malmkjaer 2005: 57), claiming that translation is an independent discipline in its own right, and rejecting the importance of linguistic studies in translation. There are, in fact, many positions that can be considered as provocatively extreme (since linguistics quite clearly does have something to offer the study of translation), such as Lederer's words (1994: 87): "I hope in this way to bring out the reasons why translation must be dealt with on a level other than the linguistic".

And nowadays, given the large number of areas with which translation overlaps, and knowing that it has benefited from input from a very wide range of fields of study, it has gained recognition as a truly interdiscipline. If we want to select another important quote representing this point of view, perhaps Neubert and Shreve's (1992: 8-10) can be fairly appropriate: "It is our firm conviction that translation is 'a house of many rooms,' and that these different rooms are often simply different discourses and perspectives on a common object of interest – translation". *Figure 2*, including a map of disciplines interfacing with Translation Studies (Hatim and Munday 2004: 8) can illustrate this interdisciplinarity.

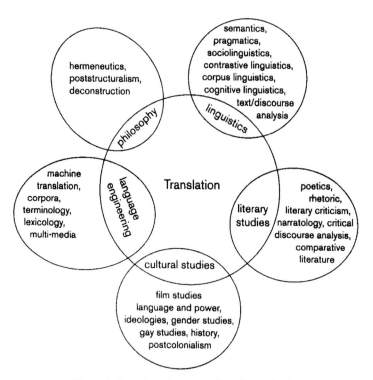

Figure 2: *Interdisciplinarity in Translation Studies.*

2.2. Approaches to Translation Studies

2.2.1. Holmes' Map of Translation Studies

Holmes' well-known paper entitled 'The Name and Nature of Translation Studies' (1972) set out to place the scholarly study of translation and was a major step forward. This map has been evolving dynamically, but it is still considered the most famous taxonomy of the main branches of study within the discipline. His conception of translation studies (extracted from Toury 1991: 181) is represented in *Figure 3*.

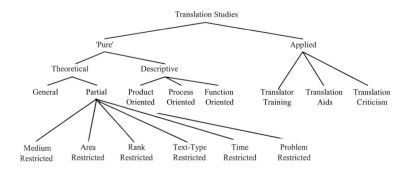

Figure 3: *Map of Translation Studies.*

As can be seen, Translation Studies is divided into two major areas: pure translation studies and applied translation studies. Pure Translation Studies deals with general translation theories and partial translation theories. The former tries to discover principles, form theories and establish models on translation. The latter, partial theoretical translation studies, can focus on the medium (written texts as opposed to oral interpreting, for instance), on the area (British culture, for example), on specific ranks or levels of analysis (syntax could be one of the levels), on different text types (like the translation of poetry), on translations from different time periods (old English into present day Spanish), and on specific problems (like the translation of formulaic language).

Descriptive Translation Studies are subdivided into product-oriented studies (focusing on the TL text, or comparative analyses of translations of the same text), process-oriented studies (focusing on how translations are done, which problems are encountered and, basically, what takes place in the translator's mind) and function-oriented studies (that try to describe the function of translations in the TL context and culture).

Applied Translation Studies, on its turn, covers translator training (dealing with teaching methods, testing techniques and curriculum planning), translation aids (like electronic tools and dictionaries), and translation criticism (like the comparison, evaluation or revision of translations). What is worth mentioning here is that the relationship between all these branches (either theoretical, descriptive or applied) should be taken into account, since each branch provides and uses insights from the others.

2.2.2. Main approaches to the study of translation

According to Malmkjaer (2005), we can talk about four main approaches to translation which have influenced translation studies: linguistic, descriptive, functional, and cultural approaches to the study of translation:

- Linguistic approaches basically refer to either theoretical models that focus on linguistic theories that concern translation, or studies that apply linguistic studies (findings, concepts, methods, etc.) to explain the task of translating. Again, we should quote Catford's ideas (1965: 1): "Translation is an operation performed on languages: a process of substituting a text in one language for a text in another. Clearly, then, any theory of translation must draw upon a theory of language – a general linguistic theory". Linguistic approaches have actually been the ones that have informed translation studies to a greater extent (for information on different linguistic approaches to translation, read chapter 4 in Malmkjaer, 2011).

- In descriptive approaches, following Holmes, studies normally describe the phenomena of translating and translations "as they manifest themselves in the world of experience" (Holmes 1988: 71). These approaches were further developed by Toury, who argued that "no empirical science can make a claim for completeness and (relative) autonomy unless it has a proper *descriptive branch*" (Toury 1995: 1), and that most translation theories to date are SL oriented, which makes the directive and normative in nature (Malmkjaer 2005), whereas we should regard translations as empirical phenomena to deal with within the culture in which they exist, following the norms that govern translation practice in the target culture, always depending on a certain geographical place and special time.

- Functional approaches, as the name indicates, see translation in terms of its function in a specific context, as a communicative act in which meaning depends on the function and the context. Thus, those following functional approaches see translation as a "purposeful transcultural activity" that always depends on the aim of the translation, with a shift of the source text to the target text and the consideration of cultural as well as linguistic factors. The German school of translation started to refer to this target of translation as the 'Skopos theory', in which translations should focus on the aim, goal, or purpose of the translation, that is actually more important in shaping the translation than the form and content of the SL text (Reiss & Vermeer 1984, Schäffner 1998, Nord 1995, ...).

- Cultural approaches started in the 1980s, when translation studies suffered a 'cultural turn' (Bassnett 1998), by means of which researchers were focusing on the importance of culture and their manifestation on languages and texts. All approaches following this cultural importance highlight the relationship between translation and other areas of study, and have derived into research on ideology, hierarchy of languages, post-colonial translation studies, gender-oriented translation studies, minority languages, political censorship, translating festivals and cultural elements, etc.

2.3. Main contribution of linguistic paradigms to the theory and practice of translation

It is particularly tempting for linguists to classify translation studies as branch of applied linguistics, as translations are linguistic phenomena. Although linguistics cannot provide all the "recipes" that are necessary to tackle the specific problems involved in translation, and other points of view indicate that language is not the only factor to take into account (see section 2.1.), it has much to offer, since a great deal of what goes on in the translation process can only be described and explained by means of linguistic studies. Indeed, if linguistics deals with language and translation also deals with languages, it seems logical to think that linguistics has something to say about translation. And, along with models and concepts imported from other fields, linguistics has consistently continued to inform studies of translation along the years.

The question is, then, which are the main contributions of linguistic theories to the study of translation? In other words, which is the impact of the various linguistic paradigms in the theory and practice of translation? We can say that research and theories on linguistics (basic assumptions, principles, methods of analysis, descriptions, attempts to provide logical, complete and comprehensive explanations of how language works, etc.) have certainly been very useful for the study of translation, and have provided a sort of formal and abstract framework for translation studies.

If we examine the main paradigms of English linguistics (traditional grammar and historical-comparative linguistics, structural linguistics, generative linguistics, functional linguistics and cognitive linguistics), assuming that readers are familiar with different research methodologies and goals within the discipline, as well as with the wide range of terminology of linguistics, we can say that all linguistic paradigms have influenced the theory and practice of translation. Here we will just list some of the main contributions, but for more details on how these theories had an impact on Translation Studies, see Fernández Guerra (2004: 59-176).

Studies within the traditional and historical paradigm influenced translation in several ways:

- The grammar-translation method was the main foreign language methodology, in which learners studied grammatical rules and vocabulary by translating sentences and texts.

- The first attempts to institutionalise translation appeared: the *House of Wisdom*, in Baghdad (IX c.), the 'Escuela de traductores de Toledo', etc.

- The two main ways of translating (literal vs. free translation) started to be discussed, mainly with Cicero (106-43 B.C.) and Saint Jerome (347-430 A.C.).

- In 1813 Schleiermacher first used the term "science of translation" (*übersetzungswissenschaft*).

- Comparative grammars and vocabulary lists in different languages established the explanatory basis for the relationships between languages, and thus were a great contribution for translators.

- The first socio-cultural approaches emerged, which influenced the reception of the translation.

- Debates and classifications of text types were proposed to guide the translator.

- Etc.

In structural linguistics, though main analysis focused not on the *use* of language ("*parole*"), but rather on the underlying abstract system of language (called "*langue*"), other major theories also had a positive effect on translation:

- The shift from diachronic (historical) to synchronic (non-historical) analysis, examining how the elements of language relate to each other in the present, synchronically, since the translator deals with texts at a specific language stage.

- Syntagmatic and paradigmatic relations that provide the linguist and the translator with a tool for categorization.

- Studies on structural relationships between words that can cause problems when translating: synonymy, polysemy, homophones, collocations, etc.

- The beginnings of modern contrastive analyses (dealing with language interference). As Alcaraz Varó y Martínez Linares (1997: 47) state, "el 'análisis de contrastes' ha constituido un instrumento metodológico útil para comparar y ordenar las dificultades estructurales dirigidas sobre todo al aprendizaje de lenguas extranjeras y de la traductología".

The important contributions of the models which emerged from generativism for linguistic analysis applied to translation can be summarized in the following lines:

- Analyses on deep and surface structures (the translator has to focus on the deep structure).

- Linguistic universals, essential to establish a proper comparison between the SL and the TL, to formulate the principle of equivalence, and to achieve the transfer of the message from the SL to the TL as accurately as possible (Nida and Taber 1969: 39).

- The set of rules which are based on a subconscious set of procedures that can be applied to *generate* sentences that are grammatical in a given language.

- The concept of linguistic competence, which would later develop into the concept of translation competence.

- The main framework of most machine translation (MT) systems was the transformational-generative grammar and the formal logic of Montague, and many MT parsers are based on a generative grammar.

The paradigm of pragmatics provided new insights in translation studies, since the ideas of 'language in action' and 'language use' had a great impact on the translation aims.

- The importance given to the context.

- The goal and audience of the translation.

- Presuppositions and implicatures in the message of a text.

- Speech acts and their different realization strategies in different languages.

- The adequacy in the translation of register and time differences (distinct historical periods), geographical differences (regional or local dialects) and social differences (social dialects or professional jargons).

- Cohesion, coherence and thematic organization of texts.

- Etc.

Nowadays, we are facing what could be called a new paradigm, in which a great amount of linguistic theories (mainly cognitivist theories) have had their counterpart in translation theory, and translations are described analysing aspects that go beyond the language (ideology, power, culture, society, etc.):

- Translation as a polysystem.

- Translation as a norm-governed activity.

- The school of manipulation.

- Deconstructive theories in Translation Studies.

- Psychological approaches to translation.

- Etc.

2.4. Further readings

Fernández Guerra, A. 2004. *Traducción inglés-español en la licenciatura en Filología Inglesa. Proyecto docente e investigador.* Castellón: Universitat Jaume I. [Chapter 5].

Holmes, J.S. 1972. The Name and Nature of Translation Studies; expanded version in *Translated! Papers on Literary Translation and Translation Studies* (pp. 66-80). Amsterdam: Rodopi, 1988.

Malmkjaer, K. 2005. *Linguistics and the Language of translation.* Edinburgh: Edinburgh University Press. [Chapter 2].

Malmkjaer, K. 2011. Linguistic approaches to translation. In Malmkjaer, K. and K. Windle (eds.) *The Oxford Handbook of Translation Studies.* Oxford: Oxford University Press. [Chapter 4].

Toury, G. 1991. What are Descriptive Studies into Translation Likely to Yield apart from Isolated Descriptions?. In van Leuven-Zwart, K. and T. Naaijkens (eds.) *Translation Studies: The State of the Art.* Amsterdam & Atlanta GA: Rodopi: 179-192.

Toury, G. 1995. *Descriptive Translation Studies and beyond.* Amsterdam & Philadelphia: Benjamins.

2.5. Tasks

1. Discuss how applied linguistics can contribute to the study of translating and translators.

2. Read again the following statement:

> It is our firm conviction that translation is a "house of many rooms", and that these different rooms are often different discourses and perspectives on a common object of interest – translation.
>
> [A. Neubert and G. Shreve (1992)]

Do you think translating is a multi-faceted activity, and that there is room for a variety of perspectives? Which ones? Why?

3. Have a look at the map of disciplines interfacing with translation studies, shown in section 2.1. It can be considered as an interdisciplinary research area, but are all those disciplines essential and closely related to the task of translating? Do you think there is any area of research missing there?

4. Translate the following passage into English. As a good translator, try to (1) reproduce, as close as possible, all the grammatical and lexical characteristics of the source text by finding appropriate equivalents in English; and (2) try to be as fluent as you can.

El paisaje de España visto por los españoles
La matanza se hace una vez al año en cada casa medianamente acomodada, y en aquella faena suele lucir la señora su actividad y tino. Se levanta antes de que raye la aurora y, rodeada de sus siervas, dirige, cuando no hace ella misma, la serie de importantes operaciones. Ya sazona la masa de las morcillas, echando en ella, con rociadas magistrales y en la conveniente proporción, sal, orégano, comino, pimienta y otras especias, ya fabrica los chorizos, longanizas, salchichas y demás embuchados. [Azorín]

5. Read the paper "Linguistic Approaches to Translation" (Malmkjaer 2011) and discuss how these approaches have contributed to the study of translation.

3. The role of the translator and translation competence

3.1. The role of the translator

Translation is a difficult activity to analyse, and so is the role of the translator. The role of a translator is to transfer a message from one language to another, but the translator also needs to address linguistic, social and cultural differences when translating, and to adapt the translation according to the aim, audience, etc. of the translation. In other words, translators are not mere walking dictionaries, they are language professionals that should take into consideration all aspects (other than the merely linguistic) that can produce different results in the translation of a text. It is difficult for a professional translator to move with the same competence from literary to scientific translation, for example, or from legal to scientific translation. Of course, the intellectual process of translation is the same, regardless the of the text to be translated, but the difference is that some texts demand specialised knowledge on specific areas (as in the case of technical and scientific translation), other text types demand knowledge of stylistic devices and literary aspects or ability to play with language (for literary texts), etc. So, which competences, or qualities, or skills, should a translator have, regardless of the text to be translated? Newmark (1995) mentions key qualities that a good translator should have: (a) reading comprehension ability in a foreign language, (b) knowledge of the subject, (c) sensitivity to language (both mother tongue and foreign language), and (d) competence to write the target language dexterously, clearly, economically and resourcefully.

There is another issue that we should question ourselves: Does the translator need to be *bilingual*? Actually, the ideal form of bilingualism is when both languages are spoken equally well for all purposes of life, interchangeably. It is easy to think that someone who speaks two languages very well is able to translate well. Unfortunately, this is not true, since translation is an awfully difficult task and very few speakers of a foreign language have the required skills to do it well. As Delisle (1988) indicates, bilingualism alone is NOT ENOUGH preparation for professional translation, and, at the same time, an active knowledge of another language is not essential to the translator, since a translator does not really need to master the SL, just to fully understand it in its written form. The reason is that, while a bilingual normally uses the knowledge of a second language to communicate orally, the translator uses that knowledge in a written text, and his or her task is not to produce, but to reformulate. In our native language, our ability to understand exceeds our ability to express ourselves when writing. The bilingual person is able to express him or herself fully in a second or foreign language, while the translator needs only to fully understand it in its written form and, thus, speaking a second language perfectly and fluently can be said to be superfluous. Translation, along these lines, consists in *writing well, in a language that one knows very well, what one has understood very well in a language that one knows well* (Delisle 1988). Obviously, a full mastery of both languages involved, excellent writing abilities in the TL across a range of styles, facility to express oneself and to write well, and experience are factors that can make this task easier because, the better the translator's command of the languages, expertise, knowledge of the fields or text types to translate…, the slighter the chance of inaccurate or poorly wordings in places or misunderstanding or interference when re-expressing the SL text.

Likewise, at all events, translation is a skill that demands an *apprenticeship*, even of a person that is truly bilingual, if he or she has not previously been trained for it. As a matter of fact, best translators and students of translation are not bilinguals. Hilaire Belloc (1931) even wondered "whether a bilingual person has ever been known to make a good translation", since "too great a familiarity with a foreign idiom may render a man confused between that idiom and his own. It may make him at times run the two together within his mind, diluting and marring each with the properties of the other". It is also worth quoting Newmark (1969: 85), who said "Any fool can learn a language, if he has enough determination to do so, but it takes an intelligent person to become a translator, and basically his work is the measure of his intelligence". The main reasons for most of the errors made by novice translators are that either they interpret the message of incorrectly or incompletely, or they are unable to re-express a passage with the appropriate words, or they are too influenced by the SL. Hence, re-expressing ideas and thoughts more easily, rapidly and accurately is definitely not easy and, as the Spanish saying recommends, "la práctica es el mejor aliado para seguir progresando".

If we analyse the role of the *translator as a reader*, we can see translation as interpretations of a text (see chapter 1). Some scholars just see the translator as the one who translates or decodes the text according to the system involved (and that it is the duty of the translator to translate what there is, and not to interpret it). But others consider that, mainly in literary works, the reader is not a *consumer*, but a *producer* of a text, who first reads and interprets in the SL and, after a process of decodification, translates the text into the TL (Bassnett 2014: 91). This seems obvious if we bear in mind that every reading is an interpretation; and the activities cannot be separated. Each translator, therefore, will produce a different version of the same text; first, because the language used can be connotative and the sense is not evident in the same way to all readers and, second, because each translator can read a different thing.

In this sense, and focusing on the translation of literary works, there are 4 essential positions of the addressee (quoted from Bassnett 2014: 90):

- Where the reader focuses on the content as matter, i.e. picks out the prose argument or poetic paraphrase, which would be completely inadequate.
- Where the reader grasps the complexity of the structure and the way in which the various levels interact, which would seem an ideal starting point.
- Where the reader deliberately extrapolates one level of the work for a specific purpose, which might be tenable in certain circumstances.
- Where the reader discovers elements that are not basic to the genesis of the text and uses the text for his own purposes, also acceptable in some cases.

As regards the method for achieving a good translation, we should look for the most reasonable one (Fernández Guerra 2000: 20). Schleiermacher pointed out that the translator has only two possible ways out:

- *To take the author to the receiver* (trying to communicate to the reader the same "impression/reaction" he experienced when reading the original; that is to say, aiming at "functional equivalence"); or
- *To take the receiver to the author* (trying to transfer the text to the reader as if the author himself had written it in the TL; retaining, as far as possible, the original's style, syntax, etc.).

Schleiermacher prefers the second; and so does Ortega y Gasset: "Traducimos en un sentido impropio de la palabra: hacemos, en rigor, una imitación o una paráfrasis del texto original. Sólo cuando arrancamos al lector de sus hábitos lingüísticos y le obligamos a moverse dentro de los del autor hay propiamente traducción. Hasta ahora casi no se han hecho más que pseudotraducciones" (Ortega y Gasset 1937). But most translators of foreign literary works have followed the opposite method, so that the reader will not realise s/he is facing a "text" in a strange language.

Whether the translation should be read as if it were an original work is a matter of debate. In English the Arnold vs. Newman debate (more than a hundred and fifty years ago) is still famous: Matthew Arnold (the poet) published the essay *On translating Homer* (1861) rejecting Newman's translation of Homer. Francis W. Newman answered back (in the same year) with his *Homeric Translation in Theory and Practice*. And Arnold replied (1862) with a new essay insisting on his point of view.

Arnold claimed that "translation must produce, on today's readers, the same effect that the original work produced on Homer's Greek readers". He was, therefore, in favour of *functional equivalence*, not giving credit to fidelity and literal exactness. Newman, on the contrary, argued that a translation "must be recognised as such"; in other words, it must be faithful to the original and not try to "re-create" it (falsifying it). Jorge Luis Borges' comments on this controversy (1957: 108-109) seem to me quite appropriate:

> La hermosa discusión Newman-Arnold, más importante que sus dos interlocutores, razonó extensamente las dos maneras básicas de traducir. Newman vindicó en ella el modo literal, la retención de todas las singularidades verbales; Arnold, la severa eliminación de los detalles que distraen o detienen, la subordinación del siempre irregular Homero de cada línea al Homero esencial o convencional, hecho de llaneza sintáctica, de llaneza de ideas, de rapidez que fluye, de altura. Esta conducta puede suministrar los agrados de la uniformidad y la gravedad; aquélla, de los continuos y pequeños asombros.

Whatever theoretical position we take, it seems that the real translator usually adopts an attitude of compromise:

(i) extreme fidelity would force him to look not only for the sense and the designation, but also for the meaning; and this is not always possible: the English saying "two heads are better than one", for example, would be in Spanish *dos cabezas son mejor que una*, rather than *cuatro ojos ven más que dos* (which is the actual "sense").

(ii) complete functional equivalence is also impossible: if we are to translate a Chinese "novel of manners", for example, we cannot change the setting, proper nouns, attitudes, etc... so as to obtain a functional equivalence in Spanish, since the message will certainly become impoverished and the novel may result in a totally new one.

Nida and Taber (1971: 31) try to solve the dilemma stating that "a translation both faithful and stylistically acceptable must be possible. Not only that, a translation which has not got as correct a style as the original [...] can't be faithful".

And García Yebra writes (1970: xxvii) what we could call a Golden rule when translating: *"La regla de oro para toda traducción es, a mi juicio,*

(1) decir todo lo que dice el original,

(2) no decir nada que el original no diga, y

(3) decirlo todo con la corrección y naturalidad que permita la lengua a la que se traduce".

Rules *(1)* and *(2)* imply *fidelity* to the original; while *(3)* allows for the necessary stylistic *freedom*. The problem, however, is to be able to apply the three rules at the same time.

3.2. Translation competence

There are many qualities a translator should have, such as knowledge of both language systems, ability to discern and analyse the meaning of a text and its form, experience in identifying possible translation difficulties, ability to express ideas well, etc. All these skills and aptitudes are normally referred to (and studied as) translator's competence, though sometimes other terms have been used, like transfer competence, translational competence, translation performance, translation ability, or translation skill. Translation competence basically refers to the underlying system of knowledge needed to translate:

> The translator's competence surpasses pure foreign language competence as acquired in foreign language classes. The translator's competence, as the ability to produce a target language text for a source language text according to certain requirements, the so-called equivalence requirements, is *qualitatively* different from the mastery of the languages involved, thus different from pure language competence. (Koller, 1992: 19-20)

We could say that, though there are many taxonomies and studies on what constitutes translation competence, most of them are not based on validated research showing the importance of those components, or necessary skills for a professional translator. The PACTE group's first objective was to provide Translation Studies with empirical research on the abilities and skills that should be considered within translation competence. Their model of translation competence is reproduced in *Figure 4* and their taxonomy includes six main elements which are interrelated (extracted from PACTE 2003: 58-60):

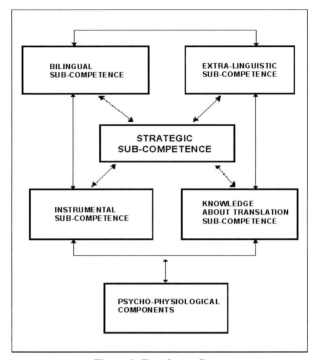

Figure 4: *Translation Competence.*

- Bilingual sub-competence, which includes procedural knowledge (pragmatic, socio-linguistic, textual, grammatical and lexical knowledge) needed to communicate in the SL and the TL.

- Extra-linguistic sub-competence, based mainly on bicultural knowledge (about both source and target cultures), encyclopaedic knowledge (about the world in general); and subject knowledge (in specialised areas or fields).

- Knowledge about translation sub-competence, on what translation is and aspects of the profession. This includes knowledge about how translation functions (types of translation methods, and types of problems plus strategies and techniques to solve them) and knowledge related to professional translation practice and the work market.

- Instrumental sub-competence, which applies to a procedural knowledge related to the use of documentation sources and translation technologies applied to translation (like dictionaries, encyclopaedias, grammars, style books, electronic corpora, etc.).

- Strategic sub-competence, or the ability to find translation problems and apply procedures to solve them.

- Psycho-physiological components, concerning different types of cognitive and attitudinal components and psycho-motor mechanisms, such as memory, perception, critical analysis, motivation, creativity, etc.

3.3. Translators' performance: TAPs

Research on translation is obviously interested in the complex process of translation and in what goes on inside the translator's mind or 'black box' whilst the translation is carried out.

The most popular experimental methods to analyse this were borrowed in the 1980s from psychology and cognitive sciences and involved 'thinking aloud protocols', which 'uses' subjects thinking aloud and verbalizing as they carry out a specific task, which then enables observers to analyse the underlying mental processes required to complete a given task, troubles, and ways to solve those problems.

In the case of translation studies, these experiments normally require participants (mainly students or professional translators) that are asked to translate a text, verbalising at the same time, all their thoughts and problems. These performances are usually recorded, transcribed, and then analysed, in order to explore and explain the psychological and linguistic mechanisms involved in the translation process and in solving translation problems.

New advances with this empirical method of research includes 'keystroke logging', which gathers data such as the number of keystrokes, corrections made, time delays, electronic dictionary look-ups, and more information that can be quite useful for the study of translation: "The rhythm and speed with which a target text was produced could then be studied as a kind of prosody of writing and reflecting the cognitive rhythm of meaning construction" (Jakobsen 2006: 96). The most common keystroke logging software are *Translog, Camtasia*, PRONIT, etc.

Although results from TAPs can be helpful in analysing the translation process and in guiding students in the acquisition of translation competence, the method has also been criticized, being the main arguments against TAPs that (1) verbalizing our thinking process is rather difficult and subjects need to be trained for it, and that (2) verbalization might interrupt and distort the translation process, thus producing unreliable facts and data (Halverson 2009: 214).

As we have seen in section 3.2., there are many skills that are useful and necessary in order to acquire translation competence, but there are many other issues to take into account when translating. The translator's brain is rather complex and has to concentrate on many factors. The image in *Figure 5* shows how some concerns affect the translation process, no matter the translator's competence.

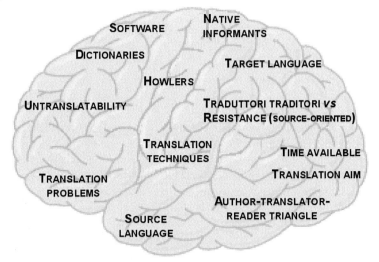

Figure 5: *The translator's brain.*

3.4. Further readings

Bernardini, S. 2001. Think-aloud protocols in translation research: Achievements, limits, future prospects. *Target* 13: 241–263.

Dechao, L. 2011. Think-aloud teaching in translation class: implications from TAPs translation research. *Perspectives: Studies in Translatology*, 19: 109-122.

PACTE. 2003. Building a Translation Competence Model. In: Alves, F. (ed.). *Triangulating Translation: Perspectives in Process Oriented Research.* Amsterdam: John Benjamins.

Rothe-Neves, R 2007. Notes on the concept of "translator's competence". *Quaderns. Revista de traducció*, 14: 125-138.

3.5. Tasks

1. Do you agree with the following statements? What are the implications for novice translators?

   (1) Bilingualism alone is NOT ENOUGH preparation for professional translation. At the same time, active knowledge of another language is NOT ESSENTIAL to the translator. The translator does not need to master the SL, but he needs to fully understand it in its written form. (J. Delisle 1988)

   (2) Translation consists in WRITING WELL, IN A LANGUAGE THAT ONE KNOWS VERY WELL, WHAT ONE HAS UNDERSTOOD VERY WELL IN A LANGUAGE THAT ONE KNOWS WELL (J. Delisle, 1988)

   (3) A bilingual may find it difficult to translate if he has not previously been trained for it. Best students are not always the so-called 'perfect bilinguals'. Hilaire Belloc even wondered "whether a bilingual person has ever been known to make a good translation". (J. Delisle, 1988)

   (4) Any fool can learn a language, if he has enough determination to do so, but it takes an intelligent person to become a translator, and basically his work is the measure of his intelligence. (P. Newmark 1969)

2. Which qualities or skills should a good translator possess? What is translation competence? Which are the main types of subcompetences within translation competence?

3. Read the articles dealing with *think aloud protocols* (in section 3.4.) and discuss the following issues:

   (a) Which are the main problems with TAP studies?

   (b) Which experiments have been made with the TAP method?

   (c) Is the adoption of this method an indication of increased interest in what actually takes place in the translators' brain when they're translating?

   (d) Can researchers be sure that translators tell them *everything*? Do TAPs really reveal the translator's thinking process?

4. Translate the passage below. You will notice something unusual (I did not transcribe it wrongly). Following the TAP method, try to verbalise all the steps you follow and everything you do (and record it).

Ulysses

Id rather die 20 times over than marry another of their sex of course hed never find another woman like me to put up with him the way I do know me come sleep with me yes and he knows that too at the bottom of his heart take that Mrs Maybrick that poisoned her husband for what I wonder in love with some other man yes it was found out on her wasnt she the downright villain to go and do a thing like that of course some men can be dreadfully aggravating drive you mad and always the worst word in the world what do they ask us to marry them for if were so bad as all that comes to yes because they cant get on without us white Arsenic she put in his tea off flypaper wasnt it I wonder why they call it that if I asked him hed say its from the Greek leave us as wise as we were before she must have been madly in love with the other fellow to run the chance of being hanged O she didnt care if that was her nature what could she do besides theyre not brutes enough to go and hang a woman surely are they

[J. Joyce]

4. Theoretical problems and controversial issues

Some of the burning, highly topical (or controversial) questions that nowadays seem to affect the theory and practice of translation are whether we should be faithful to the SL text, whether translation is actually possible, and whether we can reach equivalence, and at which levels:

(1) Fidelity vs. fluency: Should we be faithful to the SL text or do we have freedom to change and/or adapt things? To what extent are distortions allowed? For example, if we want to translate *Jo tú, Oxo está a 800 metros, ¿por qué no vamos a las tascas?,* we will find difficulty in translating formulaic expressions, cultural referents, etc. If we stay too close to the ST, readers will probably not understand all the content. But if we adapt it in order to obtain a TL text that sounds natural we will be distorting the message (*Puf! No way! The disco is half a mile away from here. Let's go pubbing instead!*)

(2) Translatability vs. untranslatability: Is translation between languages really possible? Is a good and/or perfect translation possible? Or is there always something lost in translation? When translating *Chorizos, longanizas, salchichas y demás embuchados* (section 2.5.), for instance, we probably found that there are no equivalent terms in English for all those types of sausages.

(3) Equivalence vs. adequacy: Is there exact equivalence between languages? What type of equivalence should we look for? What is the exact level of equivalence we should aim at? Again, we could show a cultural example: *Even though Christmas pudding is a traditional dessert, she's never tasted it*, in which equivalence could, depending on the aim of the translation, be reached by adapting the cultural referents: *Aunque el roscón de reyes sea un dulce típico, nunca lo ha probado.*

These are certainly old issues that have triggered off different (and, at times, antagonistic) theoretical proposals and debates. And these issues are interrelated: if there are not exact equivalents between two languages, is translation possible? Freedom and fluency in the translation can have an equivalent effect in the target culture and can, thus, make translation possible? The following sections will tackle these debates. Of course, there are other topics or big debates in translation studies, like the unit of translation (transleme, linguistic or cultural minimal units), the invariant core (basic semantic elements that be preserved in translation) or the element in translation, and many others, but they are beyond the scope of this introductory book (for more information, see Fernández Guerra, 2003).

4.1. Fidelity vs. fluency

These terms have already appeared in previous sections of this book. The reason is that this is the oldest theoretical debate in Translation Studies and represents the two opposed methods employed when translating (which, by the way, are usually said to be incompatible): *Fidelity* normally refers to faithful, literal or word-for-word translations, in which the aim is to translate accurately, without distortion, rendering the SL text's message, wording, structure, etc. *Fluency* implies free, transparent and sense translations, in which the aim is to produce a translation that appears to a native speaker of the TL to have originally been written in that language and, in some cases, also for that culture. The problem is that, in many occasions, a completely literal translation would be almost incomprehensible. Besides, at which level would we stick to? Only morphology, for example? And in a free translation, if we go too far, we can end up getting something completely new. The questions are, then, the amount of freedom we have, whether there can be a balance between a faithful and a fluent translation, and whether both qualities are necessarily mutually exclusive.

Of course, it all depends on the aim of the translation. Imagine we had to translate into Spanish the novel *The Longest Journey*, by E.M. Forster. Needless to say, there would be many differences required depending on whether the translation is intended to become a children's book (vocabulary, grammatical structures and text length would have to be simplified) or a bilingual edition for readers that know both languages and the main features of Forster's writing (the audience can compare the TL text with the SL text, and the translation should provide a fluid, yet faithful rendition of the SL text). It also depends on theoreticians and practitioners of translation, as can be observed all over the history of translation. Bassnett (1988: 39) states that "The distinction between word-for-word and sense translation, established within the Roman system, has continued to be a point of debate in one way or another right up to the present", thus evolving into numerous theories and controversies: Cicero, in the classical Roman tradition supports sense translations: *traducir non verbum pro verbo, sed sensum pro sensu.* In 17th century France, d'Ablancourt, a 17th century French critic and translator, coined the phrase *les belles infidèles* (beautiful and unfaithful), comparing women and translations, and saying that beautiful women are not faithful, and that faithful women are not beautiful. Translations known as *les belles infidèles* aimed to obtain free translations to please the reader and even improve the SL text. German and Spanish theoreticians (like Schleiermacher and Ortega y Gasset), on the contrary, advocated for faithful and literal translation (as could be read in section 3.1.).

Barbe (1999) provides an overview of the history of this debate, alluding to the most influential views on the issue. In any case, we could say that this dichotomy appears in most translation discussions and theories, even if is not overtly expressed, and if different terms are used to refer to these two ways of translating. In fact, very well-known scholars (Nida, Newmark, House, Venuti, amongst many others) have used different terminology, although the distinction appears to be quite similar:

- Formal / dynamic translation.
- Source-oriented / reader- oriented.
- Semantic / communicative translation.
- Resistance theory / Traduttore-traditore.
- Overt / covert translation.
- Documentary / instrumental translation.
- Translators (In)visibility.
- Alienating / naturalizing translation.
- Foreignisation / domestication.
- Otherness / sameness.
- Hierarchical nation and identity.
- Etc.

4.2. Translatability vs. untranslatability

These are terms used to discuss the extent to which it is possible or impossible to translate either individual words and phrases or entire texts from one language into another. As a theoretical issue, it began to be discussed in the 19th century, with the development of philosophical theories on the nature of language and communication. Well-known language philosophers (Humboldt, Sapir, Whorf and Ortega y Gasset) maintain that each linguistic community interprets reality in its own particular way, thus denying plainly any real possibility of translation between languages: Humboldt (1796) considered language as a linguistic reflection of extralinguistic reality, in a way characteristic of each individual speech community and argued that "All translation seems to me simply an attempt to solve an impossible task" (Wilss 1982: 35). His subjective idealism implies a negation of the *a priori* existence of both conceptual systems whose validity goes beyond the boundaries of individual languages, and universal principles governing the global order of extra-linguistic reality. Sapir (1929), along the same lines, asserted that "the *real world* is to a large extent unconsciously built up on the language habits of the group [...] So that the worlds in which different societies live are distinct worlds, not merely the same world with different labels attached". Similarly, Whorf (1956) abounds in Sapir's ideas, emphasising that "the limits of my language —the language I understand— mean the limits of my world". In other words, that language can only be interpreted within a culture. Finally, Ortega y Gasset (1937) expanded this point of view in the Spanish speaking world and placed the issue of untranslatability in a wider philosophical frame, which expands beyond linguistic considerations. According to Ortega y Gasset, all human actions and endeavours are essentially utopian. Therefore, the act of translating is also a utopian task: "¿No es traducir, sin remedio, un afán utópico? [...] ¿No parece la traducción, así entendida, una empresa descabellada?

At the same time, however, literary translation experienced a great upsurge, with two main tendencies: (1) *Hypertranslations* tried to improve and surpass the playful aspects, or the poetical and stylistic elements of the source text, and they reached their "peak" with the French symbolists and post-symbolists. This movement was a sort of rebirth of *les belles infidèles,* typical of the seventeenth and eighteenth centuries. (2) *Philological translations*, or the so-called philologist movement began a bit later. Philologists claimed that they (and by no means the philosophers of the language) were the only ones who should take care of translating texts (particularly those being historically old), as they could achieve the necessary metempsychosis with the author, that would enable them to apprehend the "spirit" (the essence) of the original text, and to transfer it to the target language. And some of these well-known philologists were highly praised for their translations (that appeared during the first half of the twentieth century). Both hyper-translations and philological translations could perhaps be understood as the culmination of a centuries-long tradition of interchangeability of linguistic codes. The assumption is also based on all the translations that have been done, some of them having had great influence on other people's culture and civilisation.

For abbreviation and clarity's sake, we could state that there are essentially three perspectives from which translatability has been (and still is) approached:
- Monadism: the monadic (or relativistic) approach maintains that each linguistic community interprets reality in its own particular way and this jeopardises translatability. The hypothesis claims that men's thoughts and feelings are predetermined by the various languages and cultures they are born into, and that, since no two languages are

identical, there can be no absolute correspondence between languages and thus, no fully exact translations.

- Universalism: the universalist hypothesis claims that the existence of linguistic universals ensure translatability, and says that men have common thoughts and feelings; and thus, they should have no difficulty in communicating with each other, whatever language they use (and no difficulty in transferring a message from one language into another).

- Moderate version: The polarisation of thought which the previous two opposed approaches imply has not always been manifest in translation scholarship. In fact, some theorists have oscillated between the extremes represented by universalism and monadism; and some others have attempted to combine aspects of both perspectives. Actually, what has become known as the Humboldt/Whorf/Ortega hypothesis, in its strongest formulation, seems a sort of a philosophical exercise, and would be untenable in practice, since this would imply the impossibility of effective communication between the members of different linguistic communities. And it seemed the same to a good number of Humboldt's contemporaries. In fact, communication between the members of different linguistic communities went on, goes on, and will continue to go on; and translators keep on doing their job (rendering all kinds of texts into other languages), often with a remarkable success. Consequently, a moderate version of monadism has been justified through numerous examples extracted from different (often remote) languages, in relation to kinship terminology, the semantic fields of colour, the tense configuration of verbal systems, cases in which there is no one-to-one correspondence or in which the segmentation of reality is determined by the individual languages, or the use of different referents (or "extra-linguistic reality") in sayings or proverbs of all kinds, for instance (see examples in Fernández Guerra 2012a: 40-41). As Gentzler (1993: 29) puts it: "reality can only be learned [...] through the names we give it, and so, to a certain degree, language is the creator of reality".

Acceptance of the moderate version of untranslatability presupposes that there will be terms that will vary according to their speech community, that there will be concepts which are common to two or more linguistic communities but have different connotations in each of them, and that each speech community structures reality in a different way, according to its own linguistic rules or representations of reality. All these factors have to be borne in mind when approaching the translation of any text, because they can give rise to translatability problems, but they cannot support a hypothesis of total untranslatability. That is, the impossibility of translating a text does not follow from the recognition of these circumstances. Besides, as Yifeng (2012: 231) states, the situation and aim of the translation will determine possible degrees of untranslatability:

> To create and increase translatability the variability of translational situations are directly confronted. It is thus necessary to examine the different types and degrees of untranslatability constraining and shaping translation.

Rabadán (1991: 111) established a gradation in the difficulty of translation, depending on the type and number of difficulties or gaps, all of them being a justifiable reason in favour of the moderate version of untranslatability. Such difficulties or translatability problems may be (1) of linguistic nature: polysemy, homonymy, lexical ambiguity, linguistic variants, etc.; (2) of extralinguistic nature: humour, irony, cynicism, etc.; and (3) of cultural nature: culture-specific terms. The second task in section 4.5. clearly exemplifies these three types of translatability problems.

In order to rationalise this issue, we may say (1) that absolute untranslatability of texts does not exist. And, at the same time, (2) that the perfect translation (the one which does not entail any loss from the original) is also unattainable, especially when dealing with literary translation:

(1) We can speak of *relative untranslatability* whenever we have exhausted all resources in the target language and, nevertheless, functional equivalence between source language and target language still remains beyond reach. The reasons for this can be of either a linguistic or a cultural nature. Relative linguistic untranslatability, or "*failure to find a* target language *equivalent*" (Catford, 1965: 98) occurs when the linguistic form has a function beyond that of conveying factual relationships and is therefore a constituent part of the functional equivalence to be achieved. And relative cultural untranslatability arises when a situational feature, functionally relevant for the SL text, is completely absent in the TL culture, and also when socio-cultural factors cover a different range of experience in both languages. This happens relatively often in the names of some institutions, clothes, foods and abstract concepts, amongst others.

(2) We should also speak of *relative translatability*, on the other hand, since the principle that everything can be expressed in any language is, in fact, widespread in modern linguistics. From this principle we must conclude that every text can be translated in one way or another (making recourse, when necessary, to explanatory notes, borrowings, paraphrases, etc.).

To sum up, we should try to answer two basic questions: Is translation really *impossible*? Is a *good* translation actually *possible*? The answer to the first one is NO, unless we seek a perfect reproduction with total and absolute exactness at all levels. Fortunately, translation is not this; it is rather to transfer a message from one language into another and, whenever possible, to do so displaying in the TL the same (or the most similar) stylistic features present in the SL text. Besides, effective communication between the members of different linguistic communities has certainly taken place and will continue taking place, even if that communication has not been absolutely perfect... just as, quite often, communication among members of the same linguistic community is not absolutely perfect either. The answer to the second question is YES since, from the linguistic and communicative points of view everything conceivable by the human can be expressed in any language (Kade 1964), so translation is objectively possible. Even if there are limitations, "whenever there is deficiency, terminology may be qualified and amplified by loanwords or loan-translations, neologisms or semantic shifts, and finally, by circumlocutions" (Jakobson 1966).

4.3. Equivalence vs. adequacy

The term *equivalence* appears as a solution to the dichotomies between fidelity-fluency and translatability-untranslatability, and can be considered as a *tertium comparationis* between both positions. According to Shuttleworth and Cowie (1999: 49), "the issues lurking behind the term are indeed complex and the concept of equivalence has consequently been a matter of some controversy". In fact, equivalence has been approached from different points of view:

- Some scholars (Catford, Nida and Taber, Toury, etc.) define the concept of translation in terms of equivalence relations that can exist between the SL and the TL.
- Others scholars reject the theoretical notion of equivalence, claiming it is either irrelevant (Snell-Hornby) or damaging (Gentzler) to translation studies (Kenny 2009: 96). These theorists sometimes regard translation equivalence as being only a transfer of the message from the source culture (SC) to the target culture (TC), within functionally oriented approaches to translation.
- Other scholars steer a middle course: Baker, for example, uses equivalence "for the sake of convenience, because most translators are

used to it rather than because it has any theoretical status" (Kenny 2009: 96).

In other words, we could say that positions can be radically diverse, since equivalence can be considered as a necessary condition for translation to take place, a theoretical problem in Translation Studies, or a useful category to analyse translations. These points of view have led a number of theorists to describe the notion of equivalence in several ways:

(1) Vinay and Darbelnet (1958) see equivalence as a translation procedure which "replicates the same situation as in the original, whilst using completely different wording", as in the case of idioms, animal sounds, etc.

(2) Nida y Taber (1969: 12) said that "translating consists in reproducing in the receptor language the closest natural equivalent of the source language message, first in terms of meaning and secondly in terms of style", and established two types of equivalence:

- Formal equivalence, which focuses attention on the message, both in form and content. It consists of a TL item which represents the closest equivalent of a SL term or phrase.
- Dynamic equivalence, which focuses on the principle of equivalent effect, i.e. the relationship between the receiver or message should aim to be the same as that between the original receiver and the SL message.

(3) Baker (1992) explores the notion of equivalence at different levels:

- Equivalence that can appear at word level and above word level (i.e. either in isolated terms or in phrases, idioms, etc.).
- Grammatical equivalence: diversity of grammatical categories across languages.
- Textual equivalence: in terms of information and cohesion.
- Pragmatic equivalence: implicatures and strategies of avoidance during the translation process.

(4) Kade (1968) established four types of equivalence between the SL and the TL linguistic codes:

- Type *1:1* or total equivalence, when there is full correspondence of expression and content, as in *mother → madre*, or *five → cinco*.
- Type *1:many* or optional equivalence, when there is full correspondence of content, but several significants in the TL, as in *Profesor → teacher / lecturer / professor*.

- Type *1:part* or approximate equivalence, when there is full correspondence of expression, but the TL term expresses only part of the meaning, as in *Toros → bulls*, in which the Spanish term (in its plural form) does not only denote a group of male bovine animals.
- Type *1:zero* or null equivalence, when there is no correspondence, neither at the level of content nor at the level of expression, as in the case of *gazpacho*, that could perhaps be translated as a cold tomato soup. A further distinction could be made in cases of type "1:zero". Kutz (1983), for example, distinguishes three different subtypes:

  - Denotative o referential zero-equivalence, when the SL extra-linguistic reality does not exist in the TL (nor its cognitive image). The denotative meaning of *Banderilla*, for example, as well as *banderita* (both being diminutives of *bandera*) can be translated into English as *little flag*. In a cocktail party or in the printing industry contexts, however, its denotative meaning is different; and can only be translated with periphrases such as "cocktail snacks on a stick" and "a sticker indicating a correction", respectively. But when the term is used in the bullfighting context (generally in the plural form), its denotative meaning is completely different; and the English plural *little flags* could not do, because it cannot represent the same reality.
  - Lexico-semantic zero-equivalence, when the extra-linguistic reality exists in both languages and cultures, but the cognitive segmentation of such reality is different, as in *Bank holiday, examen de selectivo, pasos, costaleros*, etc.
  - Stylistic-pragmatic zero-equivalence, when the SL stylistic devices find no reflection in the TL system. This is the case of palindromes, for instance, such as *Oirás orar a Rosario*, or *Ella te dará detalle*.

In the 1980s, however, the term equivalence as such started to be questioned: Bassnett (1980/91), for instance, says that "any notion of sameness between SL and TL must be discounted. What the translator must do is to first determine the function of the SL system and then to find a TL system that will adequately render that function". And according to Snell-Hornby (1988: 17), the view that equivalence describes the nature and the extent of relationships which exist between SL-TL texts presupposes a degree of symmetry between languages and distorts the basic problems of translation, in that it reduces the translation process to a mere linguistic exercise, ignoring cultural, textual and other situational factors (taken from Shuttleworth and Cowie 1999: 50).

Furthermore, if equal in translation meant to reproduce with total exactness, at all levels of linguistic analysis, every single piece of text or linguistic structure in the other language, then, we would certainly find it extremely difficult (if not impossible). Strictly speaking, equivalence in interlingual translation, as Roman Jakobson pointed out, is actually impossible, because there is no absolutely perfect equivalence between code units of different languages. But, fortunately (and contrary to what the term equivalence might suggest), translation is not this. Perhaps we should replace equivalence by *adequacy* (Hatim and Mason 1990, Nord 1991), because no TL text can be the formal and dynamic equivalent to a given SL text. As a rule, the term *equivalence* is, therefore, used in a relative sense, meaning the closest possible approximation to a given source text. And *adequacy* is a dynamic term used in the non-technical sense of 'adequate to the job', and refers to something which is appropriate for the communicative purpose of the translation, and adequate to a culture, a function, an audience, etc.

Dollerup (2006: 64), for example, makes a distinction between *translations as approximations* (there is no *perfect* translation or *ideal* translator and we can only discuss tangible approximations of these elusive ideals); and *adequacy* (a translation is adequate when it conveys the meaning of the source text to the TL in a given situation). Reiss and Vermeer (1984: 133), on their turn, indicate that the function of the TL text will be different depending on the aim (e.g. translations for teaching purposes and philological translations), and that the principle governing the translation process is *adequacy*. And Toury (1980) directed the attention to the TL context, distinguishing between equivalence to the SL text (*adequacy*), its ability to meet the requirements presented by the TL (*appropriacy*), and the TL reader (*acceptability*).

4.4. Further readings

Fernández Guerra, A. 2012. The issue of (un)translatability revisited: theoretical and practical perspectives. *Forum. International Journal of Translation Studies*, 10.2: 35-60.
de Pedro, R. 1999. The translatability of texts: A historical overview. *Meta*, 44: 547-559.
Barbe, K. 1996. The dichotomy free and literal translation. *Meta*, 41: 328-337.
Leonardi, V. 2000. Equivalence in Translation: Between Myth and Reality. *Translation Journal*, vol. 4, No. 4.

4.5. Tasks

1. Discuss the following issues:

- Explain the assumptions supporting quotes (a), (b) and (c).

- According to quotes (d), (e) and (f), there are only two possible ways out for the translator. Which ones?

- How and why did these statements influence Translation Studies?

(a) Todos estamos en poder de la lengua que hablamos; nosotros, y todo nuestro pensamiento, somos producto de ella; no podemos pensar con total precisión nada que esté fuera de sus fronteras. [...] ¿No parece la traducción, así entendida, una empresa descabellada? (Schleiermacher 1813)

(b) Pero ¿es esto posible? ... ¿no se le está pidiendo (a la lengua terminal) algo imposible? (Rosenzweig 1924)

(c) Con frecuencia se ha advertido [...] que [...] ninguna palabra de un idioma se corresponde perfectamente con otra de otro idioma. (Humbold 1816)

(d) Hay dos máximas para traducir: la primera pretende que el autor de una nación extranjera sea traspuesto a la nuestra de tal manera que podamos considerarlo como maestro; la otra, por el contrario, exige de nosotros que nos trasladamos a su figura, que nos situemos en sus circunstancias, su manera de decir y sus peculiaridades. (Goethe 1813)

(e) O bien el traductor deja al escritor lo más tranquilo posible y hace que el lector vaya a su encuentro, o bien deja lo más tranquilo posible al lector y hace que vaya a su encuentro el escritor. Ambos son tan por completo diferentes, que uno de ellos tiene que ser seguido con el mayor rigor, pues cualquier mezcla produce necesariamente un resultado muy insatisfactorio [...]. (Schleiermacher 1813)

(f) Traducimos en un sentido impropio de la palabra: hacemos, en rigor, una imitación o una paráfrasis del texto original. Sólo cuando arrancamos al lector de sus hábitos lingüísticos y le obligamos a moverse dentro de los del autor hay propiamente traducción. Hasta ahora casi no se han hecho más que pseudotraducciones. (Ortega y Gasset 1937)

2. Translate the following passages. You will notice that there are several linguistic, extra-linguistic and cultural *untranslatable* elements. Remember that translation equivalence can be reached at all levels, since it is a

functional concept that can be attributed to any particular translational situation.

More traps and less tricks

(1) Just because I am chased don't get the idea I am chaste.

(2) Why is six afraid of seven? Because 7, 8, 9.

(3) Are you training for a race? No I'm racing for a train.

(4) Why are Egyptian children good children? Because they respect their mummies.

(5) Sin tu ayuda, SIDA; con tu ayuda, VIDA.

(6) A waiter? Why do they call those food servers *waiters*, when it's the customers who do the waiting?

(7) I've had many womantic relationships over my life.

(8) He sacado al balcón los zapatos y un plato de churros para cuando vengan los Reyes. Tú no hace falta que los saques porque el carbón te lo pueden dejar en cualquier parte.

(9) A la chica le dio su abuela una perra chica de propina, por ser tan mona; pero su madre estaba hecha un basilisco y dijo que darle tanto no se le hubiera ocurrido ni al que asó la manteca. No sólo eso, le salía humo por las orejas porque aquel pequeño demonio no se había portado bien; eran ya casi las tres y aún no había preparado la comida. Como suele decirse, hágase, haga, y nadie comenzaba; unos por otros, la casa sin barrer... y la fabada sin hacer.

(10) *Camarero*:   — ¿Qué desea?
       Pepita: —¿Me pone un gazpacho?
       Camarero: — Yo de todo te doy.

3. How faithful should we be (or can we be) when we translate?
   Discuss the notions of *literal* and *free* translation and the merits of each.

4. Describe the main approaches to (un)translatability. What do you think about the issue?

5. Exemplify the main types of equivalences between two different languages [please note that Kade's, Kutz's and Rabadán's taxonomies are very important!].

6. Read V. Leonardi's article "Equivalence in Translation: Between Myth and Reality" and answer the following questions:

   (a) Which are the main classifications of the term *equivalence*? List and describe the main types of equivalence.

   (b) The term equivalence has caused, and it seems quite probable that it will continue to cause, heated debates within the field of translation studies. Why?

   (c) Catford's approach to translation equivalence clearly differs from that adopted by Nida. Why?

   (d) At which levels does Baker explore the notion of equivalence?

   (e) Do you think that equivalence is used for the sake of convenience, because most translators are used to it rather than because it has any theoretical status?

   (f) Now that you've seen so many definitions and taxonomies, how would you define translation equivalence? Can you establish your own classification?

7. Translate the text below into Spanish. Please note that

   - A translation should sound as if it never existed in a foreign language;
   - The concept 'translation unit' normally refers to the SL unit which can be recreated in the TL without addition of other meaning elements from the SL;
   - The text is full of idioms, and *the ideal* is to transfer into the TL the same sense, designation and literal meaning.

Weird (though 'possible') text

The average Spaniard sleeps like a log, eats like a horse and has the eyes of a lynx, but he leads a dog's life.
In order to be able to take the rough with the smooth, he has to be as cunning as a fox. Though love, which is often his favourite occupation, can make him walk on the air, happy as a lark, he doesn't like to be taken

for a sucker or be led up the garden path. So, if the 'birds' stand him up too often, especially in a weather that would skin you alive, he soon gets hot under the collar and, far from beating about the bush, he will take the bull by the horns; because, though he sometimes plays dumb to get what he wants, he's nobody's fool.

He may get sick as a dog, with a hell of a fever, but he will manage to keep a stiff upper lip; for, if he can talk his head off, he also knows how to remain, if need be, as silent as a tomb.

Admit he's a queer fish.   [Daninos]

5. Translation strategies and techniques

5.1. Methods, techniques, procedures and strategies

The way in which we translate either individual words and phrases or entire texts has been assigned a multitude of labels, among which we have 'procedures', 'techniques', 'strategies', 'processes', 'methods', etc. These terms are sometimes (wrongly) used as synonyms by some people but, following Molina and Hurtado (2002), we should distinguish between translation methods, techniques, strategies and procedures:

Translation *method* is a wide term that refers to the way a particular translation process is carried out, normally in terms of the aim of the translation. It is an overall method we apply to a text as a whole and the primary choice here is how close to the SL text we want the TL text to be. Newmark (1988) lists the following translation methods: word-for-word translation, literal translation, faithful translation, semantic translation, communicative translation, idiomatic translation, free translation, and adaptation. This overall method we chose will affect the way we translate individual words and phrases or, in other words, the technique we employ.

Translation *strategy*, in line with Krings (1986) or Lorscher (1991), could be defined as the conscious or unconscious procedures leading to the optimal solution of a translation problem. The way in which we solve those problems, again, depends on the technique we employ. These problem solving strategies can be used for comprehension, in order to distinguish main ideas, establish conceptual relationships, or search for information, and also apply for the production or reformulation of the text, including paraphrase, retranslate, say out loud, or avoiding words that are close to the original (Molina and Hurtado 2002: 508). When dealing with production strategies, Chesterman (1997), for instance, mentions syntactic strategies (that involve purely syntactic changes and manipulating form), semantic strategies (concerning lexical semantics), and pragmatic strategies (dealing with the selection of information in the TL text, and including cultural or linguistic changes).

Finally, a translation *technique*, is the result of the choice we make when we translate specific items of the SL text, and could be defined as a procedure used to analyse and classify equivalence issues in our translation. As stated by Molina and Hurtado (2002: 509), they have five basic characteristics:

techniques affect the result of the translation, they are classified by comparison with the original, they affect micro-units of text, they are by nature discursive and contextual, and they are functional.

When describing translation techniques, or evaluating the use of one or another technique, though, we need to be cautious, since all possible techniques and procedures have to be considered within a particular context, not in isolation. The appropriateness of using a particular technique will depend on several aspects, such as text type (a poem or a scientific paper), the aim of the translation (a bilingual edition or just a draft translation for someone who does not understand the SL), the mode of the translation (written translation, sight translation, or oral interpretation), etc.

5.2. Taxonomies of translation techniques

There are different taxonomies that try to describe translation techniques. In any case, these procedures or techniques that are usually mentioned in translation manuals and some scholarly publications serve both to analyse and catalogue translation equivalence and to improve the acquisition of translation competence, since knowing and comparing them is definitely necessary to produce an adequate translation. As Malone (1988: 2) indicates, such techniques or procedures "will serve either as tools for the study of completed translation (the analytic mode), or as helpmates in the act of translation (the operative mode)". One of the leading taxonomies, and certainly the best known, is that of Vinay and Dalbernet (1977). They propose seven basic translation procedures: adaptation, calque, equivalence, modulation, borrowing, literal translation and transposition; although they also refer to compensation, expansion and contraction. Other authors have reformulated and added new procedures, or broken down the aforementioned ones into distinct subcategories. Among the well-known reformulations we should mention the one proposed by Vázquez Ayora (1977), for example, who distinguishes between (i) oblique translation procedures (adaptation, amplification, compensation, equivalence, explicitation, modulation, omission and transposition) and (ii) direct methods (calque, loan and literal translation). Hurtado (2001: 268-271) expands the list with strategies that account for solutions of textual nature: extension, amplification, compression, discursive creation, description, generalisation, particularisation, reduction, paralinguistic or linguistic substitution, and variation.

Among all the prescriptive approaches, Newmark's (1988: 81-91), which specifically addresses the translation of cultural elements, remains one of the most representative ones. Newmark proposes the procedures of literal translation, transference, naturalization, cultural equivalent, functional equivalent, descriptive equivalent, componential analysis, synonymy, through-translation, shifts or transpositions, modulation, recognized translation, compensation, and paraphrase. He also includes couplets (combination of two or more different procedures), and refers to the importance of notes in order to account for differences between SL and TL cultures.

Graedler (2000: 3), for her part, lists four main procedures for translating cultural terms: (1) making up a new word, (2) explaining the meaning of the SL expression in lieu of translating it, (3) preserving the SL term intact, and (4) replacing it using any term in the TL that has the same "relevance" as the SL term.

Harvey (2003: 2-6) also proposes four ways out: (1) functional equivalence, using a term with the same "function", (2) formal or linguistic equivalence, or word by word translation, (3) transcription or borrowing, which may include notes, and (4) descriptive or self-explanatory translation.

Mur Dueñas (2003: 74-79) labelled her translation procedures as (1) TL cultural cognate; (2) SL cultural and linguistic borrowing; (3) SL cultural borrowing plus explanation; (4) replacement of SL cultural referent by explanation; (5) TL cultural referent suppression; and (6) literal translation of TL cultural referent.

Marco Borillo (2004: 148), considering the intervention of the translator and his approach to the TC as a continuum, proposes the following six procedures: (1) pure or naturalised loan, (2) literal translation, (3) neutralisation (description, generalisation or particularisation), (4) amplification or compression, (5) intracultural adaptation, and (6) intercultural adaptation.

Finally, Fernández Guerra (2012b: 126) established a taxonomy including seven procedures ranging from those techniques that focus more on the source culture (SC) to those that try to adapt the translation to target culture (TC) readers. These are represented in *Figure 6*.

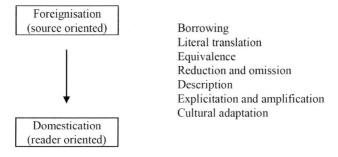

Figure 6: *Procedures to translate cultural terms.*

All these procedures mentioned are, according to many experts, the main translation techniques that could be used when dealing with problems that students can face in translating texts. Jääskeläinen, for example, considers that the strategies used by a translator are skills and procedures that promote the acquisition and use of information, and may be associated both with the product (the translated text), as well as with the process of translation itself, whose strategies "are a set of (loosely formulated) rules or principles which a translator uses to reach the goals determined by the translating situation" and can be global or local strategies: "global strategies refer to general principles and modes of action and local strategies refer to specific activities in relation to the translator's problem-solving and decision-making" (Jääskeläinen 2005: 16).

5.3. Description of fifteen translation techniques

All the aforementioned techniques will now be briefly described and illustrated, in alphabetical order:

(1) Adaptation

Adaptation is used in those cases in which the type of situation being referred to by the SL message is unknown in the TC and translators create a new situation that can be described as a situational equivalence (Vinay and Darbelnet 1977: 52-53). Thus, it can be understood as what other authors have called cultural, dynamic or functional equivalence. It actually refers to a SL cultural element that is replaced by another term in the TC. This would apply, for example, to *Christmas pudding,* and its possible translation into 'turrón' mentioned above. There are situations in which adaptation seems, to some extent, necessary: in advertising slogans, or children's stories, for example. In other cases there are certain conventions, more or less generalized, as regards adapted translations of foreign cultural elements in the TL. This applies, for instance, to weights and measures, musical notation, generally accepted titles of literary works or geographical names, etc. The basic goal of the translator when trying to 'adapt' the translation is to get a similar effect on the TL readers, 'domesticating', in a way, the cultural terms.

(2) Borrowing

Borrowing a term is taking a word or expression straight from another language, without being translated. The procedure is normally used when a term does not exist in the TC, or when the translator tries to get some stylistic or exotic effect. It can be "pure", if there is no change of any kind in the foreign term (*broker, chip, clown, feeling, stop*, etc.), or "naturalized", if the word has some change in the spelling, and perhaps some morphological or phonetic adaptation (as in *diskette* → 'disquete', *format* → 'formatear', *indent* → 'indentar', *reset* → 'resetear', etc.). Some authors prefer the terms *foreign word, foreignism, Anglicism, Germanism,* ... when referring to pure borrowings (that have not been fully assimilated into the TL system), and use borrowings or loans when the words are naturalised in the TL, the difference being when the term has been incorporated and how it has been adapted to the TL (Torre 1994: 94). In any case, borrowings are one of the main ways of enriching a language, as the Spanish writer Unamuno indicated as regards literary translation: "meter palabras nuevas, haya o no haya otras que las reemplacen, es meter nuevos matices de ideas" (cf. Lorenzo 1981). And, as far as English is concerned, Wagner states that it is "the only language whose elements are seventy-five percent of foreign origin" (cf. Fernandez 1993: 514). When translating texts with a great amount of cultural terms, however, we should be cautious (García Yebra 1982: 340), unless we want to maintain a certain local colour or exoticism.

(3) Calque

Calque could be described as a literal translation (either lexical or structural) of a foreign word or phrase. It could actually be considered a special type of loan or borrowing, since the translator borrows the SL expression or structure and then transfers it in a literal translation (Vinay and Darbelnet 1977: 47), as in the case of *shocked* → 'chocado', *stressed* → 'estresado', etc. The difference between loan/borrowing and calque is that the former imitates the morphology, signification and phonetics of the foreign word or phrase, while the latter only imitates the morphological scheme and the signification of that term, but not its pronunciation. In the case of *football*, for example, using the same term in Spanish would be a pure borrowing, the word *fútbol* would be a naturalised borrowing, and *balompié* a calque. According to Santoyo (1987: 93), calque is not only an acceptable form of translation, it is strict and correct translation, since it is built with significants of the SL. García Yebra (1982: 335) also considers that it leads to a good translation and that it can certainly contribute to enrich the TL (whereas borrowings are, according to him, not really translation procedures, but a way of giving up in the translation task).

(4) Compensation

The aim of compensation is to balance the semantic losses that translation involves (either in the content of the message or its stylistic effects).

Compensation introduces a SL element of information or stylistic effect in another place in the TL text because it cannot be reflected in the same place as in the SL: the translation of dialects, irony, politeness values, etc. In the case of Spanish-English translation, we could mention, for example, the familiarity or formality of "tú" and "usted". Both words are translated into English as "you", so the translator will have to express degrees of formality in different ways, maybe compensating by using other English words of the formal and informal registers, in order to preserve the same level of formality.

(5) Compression / reduction / condensation / omission

These four terms are opposed to the ones mentioned under (8) Explicitation / expansion / amplification / diffusion. In all of them the translator synthesizes or suppresses a SL information item in the TL text, mainly when that information is considered unnecessary (Vázquez Ayora 1977: 359) because the cultural term does not perform a relevant function or may even mislead the reader. Compression/reduction/condensation/omission of information is not common when translating cultural terms and, when it occurs, it is normally to avoid repetitions, misleading information, or lack of naturalness.

(6) Description

As the term itself indicates, a term or expression is replaced by a description of its form or function. It could, thus, be regarded as a sort of paraphrase, or even as an amplification or explanation of a SL term, as in the Spanish translation of *He's a Cockney* → 'Es de la parte este de Londres, de la parte más pobre'.

(7) Equivalence

According to Vinay and Dalbernet, equivalence refers to a strategy that describes the same situation by using completely different stylistic or structural methods for producing equivalent texts (Vinay and Dalbernet 1977: 52). This basically means that the translator uses a term or expression recognised as an established equivalent in the TL. It is similar to adaptation and to modulation in that it expresses the same situation in a different way (Vázquez Ayora 1977: 322), mainly in cases of idioms and formulaic language, as in *God bless you* → '¡Salud!', *Holy cow!* → '¡Madre mía!', *You must be joking!* → '¡Ni hablar!', *Only the good die young* → 'Mala hierba nunca muere'.

(8) Explicitation / expansion / amplification / diffusion

These terms are in opposition to *compression / reduction / condensation / omission*. Explicitation means that we express in the TL something that is implicit in the context of the SL (Vázquez Ayora 1977: 349), or that we introduce details that are not expressed in the SL, such as more information, translator's notes, or explicative paraphrasing, as in the translation of *IRA* as 'La organización terrorista IRA'. In the other three cases, those of expansion (Vinay and Darbelnet 1977: 184), amplification (Vazquez Ayora 1977: 137) and diffusion (Malone 1988: 45), the translator uses, in the TL, more words than in the SL to express the same idea. Examples of these procedures could be the following ones: *Coffee break* → 'descanso para tomar café', *The man next door* → 'el hombre que vive (en la puerta de) al lado', *Successful fishermen went back home* → 'los pescadores que habían tenido éxito volvieron a casa'.

(9) Generalization

With this procedure, in opposition to particularisation, the translator uses hypernyms or more general or neutral terms, normally for stylistic reasons, or also to avoid unnecessary repetitions or ambiguity, as in the case of *John has a beautiful dog* → 'Juan tiene un hermoso *animal*'.

(10) Literal translation

Literal translation, or word by word, occurs when a SL word or phrase is translated into a TL word or phrase, without worrying about style, but adapting the text to the TL syntactic rules, with minimal adjustments, so that it sounds both correct and idiomatic (word order, functional words, etc.). In Vinay and Dalbernet's words (1977: 48), it is the direct transfer of a SL text into a grammatically and idiomatically appropriate TL text in which the translators' task is limited to observing the adherence to the linguistic servitudes of the TL. An example of literal translation could be *John loves Mary* as 'Juan ama a María', in which the preposition 'a' has been added because it is a requirement for direct objects denoting person.

(11) Modulation

Modulation consists of using a phrase that is different in the SL and the TL to convey the same idea (Vinay and Dalbernet 1977: 51). In other words, there is a change in the point of view, focus, perspective or category of thought in relation to the SL, as in *Neither head nor tail* as 'ni pies ni cabeza', *Don't get so excited* as 'tranquilízate', ... It is similar to transposition and, sometimes, necessary in order to avoid lack of fluency or exoticism in the translation.

(12) Particularisation

Particularisation is opposed to generalisation. It refers to the procedure in which the translator uses in the TL hyponyms or more precise or concrete terms, as in *She's a great person* for 'Es una mujer maravillosa', in which particularisation disambiguates whether 'person' is male or female, since there is no translation of 'she' in this case.

(13) Substitution (linguistic-paralinguistic)

According to Hurtado (1999: 36), linguistic-paralinguistic substitution is the translation procedure in which linguistic elements are replaced by paralinguistic elements (intonation, gestures, etc.) or vice versa, as in *Oh, what a shame!,* which could perhaps be translated as '¡Qué pena!– dijo sorprendida', or to translate the Arab gesture of putting your hand on your heart as 'Thank you'.

(14) Transposition

This procedure involves changing a grammatical category or replacing one part of the speech for another, without changing the meaning of the message (Vinay and Dalbernet 1977: 50). The following translations are types of transposition: *This computer is out of order* as 'Este ordenador no funciona', *I knocked him down* as 'Le derribé de un golpe', *I touched a footbrake* as 'Frené'... (this last example also includes a reduction). Grammatical transpositions, with appropriate morphological and syntactic adjustments, are quite frequent in order to obtain a translation that sounds as if it had been originally written in the TL.

(15) Variation

Finally, variation is a procedure in which the translator changes elements that affect several aspects of linguistic variation: changes in tone, style, social dialect, geographical dialect, ... (Hurtado 1999: 37), as in the case of *I ain't no fool* for 'No soy ningún tonto', or in *Yep, and it's dirt cheap* for 'Sí, y se lo dejo muy barato', in which the register used in the TL is completely different.

5.4. Further readings

Fernández Guerra, A. 2012b. Crossing Boundaries: The Translation of Cultural Referents in English and Spanish. *Word and Text. A Journal of Literary Studies and Linguistics*. Vol. II: 121-138.

Marco Borillo, J. 2004. Les tècniques de traducció (dels referents culturals): retorn per a quedar-nos-hi. *Quaderns. Revista de traducció* 11: 129-149.

Molina, L. and A. Hurtado Albir. 2002. Translation Techniques Revisited: A Dynamic and Functionalist Approach. *Meta, XLVII, 4*: 498-512.

5.5. Tasks

1. Here are eight sentences, together with a possible translation. Which technique has been used in each case?

    (1) Tu novio es un cabrón. → Your boyfriend is a bastard.

    (2) His sense of humour is obvious. → Su sentido del humor es obvio.

    (3) El jefe está trabajando para acabar el informe. → The boss is working to finish the report.

    (4) She likes running. → Le gusta correr.

    (5) –Ey, jefe, que mañana no vengo– dijo Quique. → "Hey boss, I'm not coming tomorrow" said Quique, in a quite over-familiar way.

    (6) The sound of music. → Sonrisas y lágrimas.

    (7) Me gusta el gazpacho. → I like gazpacho.

    (8) Quality assurance is unnecessary. → El aseguramiento de calidad es innecesario.

2. Suggest suitable translations into Spanish for all the sentences below. Whenever possible, offer several translations for each, using at least two different procedures or strategies (feel free to use your imagination):

    (1) He was seen yesterday, while he was having lunch.

    (2) Oh! Don't be silly!

    (3) She hates Christmas pudding.

    (4) The Signora wears a mantilla after her siesta.

    (5) Oh, what a shame! I'm soooooooo amazed!

(6) Holy cow! He's a Cockney.

(7) Cockney. Cockneys. Cock. Knees. Why do men from London get stiff in the legs?

(8) I got this fridge from the Salvation Army.

(9) Te dejo ya, que Mercadona cierra a las 10 y aún tengo que comprar lo de los calimochos.

(10) Mi compi Leonor es fallera mayor y mi prima Rocío siempre va al Rocío; por eso, tras la procesión, siempre van de botellón.

3. Find three words or phrases in English that you consider difficult to translate into Spanish. Exchange them with your partner and try to render his/her words into Spanish.

4. Translate one of the following passages into English and note which translation strategies you consider better suited for this task (according to the context). Later, compare your translation with others who have worked on the same passage and consider their degree of faithfulness or literality.

(a) Un cojo, que enseñaba a la caridad de las gentes un muñón bastante asqueroso, pedía limosna a gritos al lado de un tenderete de rosquillas; de vez en vez caía alguna perra y entonces el cojo se la tiraba a la rosquillera.

– ¡Eh! – le gritaba –. ¡De las blancas!

Y la rosquillera, que era una tía gorda, picada de viruela, con los ojos pitañosos y las carnes blandengues y mal sujetas, le echaba por los aires una rosquilla blanca como la nieve vieja, sabrosa como el buen pan del hambre y dura como el pedernal. Los dos tenían bastante buen tino.

(b) Cuando la familia se puso en marcha, en el camino de vuelta al pueblo, el astro rey se complacía en teñir de color de sangre unas nubecitas alargadas que había allá lejos, en el horizonte.

– Me canso.

– ¡Aguántate! También nos cansamos los demás y nos aguantamos. ¡Pues estaría bueno!

– Yo no quiero meterme en nada, allá vosotros; pero yo siempre os dije que me parecía una barbaridad grandísima meter a los niños semejante caminata en el cuerpo.

(c) Luisito, después de mucho pensarlo, se acercó a su madre, zalamero como un perro cuando menea la cola:

– Mamá, ¿me dejas jugar con esos niños?

La madre miró para el grupo y frunció el ceño:

– ¿Con esos bárbaros? ¡Ni hablar! Son todos una partida de cafres.

(d) Los demás tenían bastante sed, pero se la tuvieron que aguantar porque la botella de la vieja era tabú – igual que una vaca sagrada – y fuente no había ninguna en dos leguas a la redonda. En realidad, habían sido poco precavidos, porque cada cual podía haberse traído su botella; pero, claro está, a lo hecho, pecho: aquello ya no tenía remedio y, además, a burro muerto, cebada al rabo.

5. Translate the passages below into Spanish.

- Which problems did you encounter when translating?
- Were these due to differences between both linguistic systems?
- What about historical and cultural elements?
- Did you make recourse to any translation technique or strategy in order to solve those problems?

Eureka Street

I turned right into Beechmount. Beechmount looked like Beechmount always looked - small, unprosperous. Little terraced houses with little terraced people standing on the doorsteps. Some kids ran about the pavement as they always did and some broken glass lay around as was habitual. The walls were painted with a variety of crude scenes depicting how much nicer Catholics were than Protestants and a series of inventive tableaux in which large numbers of British soldiers were maimed and killed. These were the Belfast mean streets, the internationally famous and dreaded West Side jungle. It was no big deal. The scorbutic children and big mamas were stock stuff. You could see worse in any city. Even as nearby as Dublin and London you could find more dramatic poverty, more profound deracination. You mightn't come across the same quality of Armalites but everything else would look much the same.

[R. McLiam Wilson]

What's For Breakfast, Lunch and Dinner? British Food & Drinks

Is it really true that 'English food is tasteless and greasy'? You can, of course, still order fish and chips at the local pubs or take-aways. Fish and chips are served over the counter wrapped in paper, and traditionalists prefer to eat them straight out of the paper because they taste better that way!

What do ales, beers and tea have in common? They are so called "national drinks" in the UK. Most British people enjoy a "nice cup of tea" or a pint (of beer). Tea with milk and beer without a head. The British would think that they had been given short measure if there was a large head at the top of their glass of beer. About one finger thick is enough. It's all a matter of taste.

Britain is a tea-drinking nation. Most Britons like their tea strong and dark, but with a lot of milk, but they do drink coffee as well, either freshly-made or instant.

Sometimes it seems that they're always drinking tea. Don't misunderstand them when they say 'We are having our tea'. This doesn't mean they're drinking a cup of tea. It means they are having their evening meal or supper.

A typical British meal for dinner is meat and "two veg". Gravy covers the meat, and one of the vegetables is almost always potatoes. However, this meal is rarely eaten nowadays; a recent survey found that most people in Britain are eating curry! Rice or pasta are now favoured as the 'British Dinner'. On Sundays the main meal of the day is often eaten at midday instead of in the evening. This meal usually is a Roast Dinner consisting of roast beef, Yorkshire pudding and two kinds of vegetables.

More recently, the British diet has been enriched by the vast array of ethnic foods available in our shops and restaurants, and due to the great mixture of ethnic groups throughout the UK, you can find Indian restaurants and Balti houses, Mediterranean cuisine, as well as Chinese and Lebanese restaurants. Kebab and falafel stands abound, often outselling their Western fast-food competition through larger portions and later hours.

6. Practical problems in English-Spanish translation

6.1. Classifying problems in translation

Translating always involves practical problems and difficulties. There are many classifications of problems that can be analysed when translating. As Hale and Campbell (2002: 14) indicate "the notion of difficulty in translation is elusive and prone to subjective judgement". Reiss (1982: 12), for instance, analysed four levels of text difficulty focusing on five aspects that could pose some problems, as shown in *Figure 7*.

	1st level of difficulty	2nd level of difficulty	3rd level of difficulty	4th level of difficulty
Subject matter	General Transcultural	General Culture specific	Specialised Transcultural	Specialised Culture specific
Register	Educated	Colloquial	Technical Sociolects	Individual
Type of language use	Informative	Informative-evocative	Evocative	Persuasive
Pragmatics of the reader	Universal	Collective	Group	Individual
Historical-cultural context	Close temporally and culturally	Close culturally but distant temporally	Distant culturally and close temporally	Distant culturally and temporally

Figure 7: *Levels of text difficulty.*

Nord (1991: 59-60) categorised translation problems according to four different types, which require specific transfer strategies:

- Pragmatic translation problems: differences between the situations in the SC and the TC. These differences include time, place, text function, audience, etc.

- Intercultural translation problems: differences in norms and conventions that guide verbal and non-verbal behaviour in the two cultures involved, as every culture has its own habits and conventions.
- Interlingual translation problems: differences of structure in the vocabulary, syntax and suprasegmental features of the SL and TL.
- Text-specific translation problems: They are the ones that cannot be included in any of the other three categories. They refer to specific situations of communication that are unique and depend on a certain specific text and whose solution cannot be generalised. In this category we find the translation of puns, metaphors, similes, rhetorical figures, etc.

Fernández Guerra (2014: 164) analysed, among several other issues, the most problematic aspects of translation that students encountered when translating from English into Spanish and vice versa and eight categories of translation problems were devised:

- Linguistic problems: problems due to differences between both linguistic systems.
- Text type problems: specific function of the text, subject-matter, etc.
- Cultural problems: culture-specific terms, differences between cultures, etc.
- Stylistic problems: translating poetry, puns, humour, metaphors, etc.
- Register problems: formal language, colloquial language, dialects, sociolects, and any other deviation from standard language.
- Historical-temporal problems: historical issues, texts that are temporally distant, etc.
- Lack of resources: dictionaries, encyclopaedias, style books, etc.
- Time available: not enough time to carry out the task.

Finally, Campbell (1999) mentioned that difficult items in a SL text are those that require more processing effort to resolve TL choices and suggested three main factors that affect translation difficulty:

- SL text difficulty.
- Translator competence.
- Translation task type.

The tasks included in section 6.5. include all these abovementioned potential sources of translation difficulty, focusing on some specific problematic elements that can cause problems in English-Spanish translation:

- Differences between both linguistic systems.

- Text typology.
- Indirect translation.
- Translating culture.
- Literary translation.

6.2. Problems in English-Spanish translation

6.2.1. Differences between both linguistic systems

There are many differences between English and Spanish, at all levels (phonology, grammar, vocabulary, realisation of speech acts, politeness values, typographical conventions, etc.). However, these differences should not pose a problem for a translator (with high communicative competence in the foreign language, who should avoid negative transfer or interference from the native language), it should just present problems for the language learner. Here are some examples:

- Pronunciation difficulties: both sound systems are certainly different. Spanish has 5 vowel sounds and 5 diphthongs, whereas with English has 12 pure vowel sounds and 8 diphthongs, and the length of the vowel is quite significant in distinguishing between words. Consonants can also cause problems for Spanish speakers, since some English phonemes have no equivalent sound in Spanish. Besides, intonation patterns can also be different, since English is generally categorised as a stress-timed language and Spanish is usually considered to be a syllable-timed language.

- Vocabulary difficulties: English and Spanish have many cognates, and thus many false friends, such as *actually* (which should be translated as 'en realidad', and not as 'actualmente'), *assist* ('ayudar', not 'asistir'), *casualty* ('herido', not 'casualidad'), etc.

- Grammar Difficulties: There are many grammatical differences that can cause difficulties for a language learner. A main difference is the tense and form of the verbs. Spanish is a much more heavily inflected language than English and there is no one-to-one correspondence in the use of the tenses, as in: *What are you doing?* (*¿Qué hace(s)?*) or · *I had breakfast* (*He desayunado*). Word order can also lead to confusion, because Spanish allows much more flexibility than English (*The students in his class can't write* could be translated as *No pueden escribir los alumnos de su clase*, for example). Other important differences can be found in the use of articles (*He is a lawyer* for *Es* *abogado*, *British colonies* for *Las colonias británicas*), adjectives (*Viste siempre corbata y camisa de seda* for *He always wears silk shirt and tie*), posesives (*He had his hands clean* for *Tenía las manos limpias*), personal pronouns (*When she talks, she smiles* for *Cuando habla sonríe*), etc.

For more differences between English and Spanish, see López Guix and Wilkinson (1997). Still, as mentioned above, when the translator has the necessary communicative competence and knowledge of the rules of the languages involved, knows how language is used for communicative purposes, and is able to write and express things well, these differences should not be a drawback. There are some other differences, though, that may cause problems for the translator, especially when the different levels of linguistic analysis interact, as in the case of ambiguity, polysemy, wordplays, humour, metaphor, sound, etc.

6.2.2. Text type in translation

Translation theorists have proposed different translation taxonomies for text types and functions. The first classifications of text typologies and functions that could guide the translator started within the traditional and historical linguistic paradigm. But moving on to the most relevant typologies for Translation Studies, we should mention the three types established by Reiss (1976), based on Bühler's terms *Darstellung, Ausdruck, Appell* (Bühler 1934), establishing a correlation between text type, translation method and translation function:

- Informative texts, in which the translator should focus on semantic relationships within the text and only secondarily on connotative meanings and aesthetic values.
- Expressive texts, where the aim is to try and preserve aesthetic effect alongside relevant aspects of the semantic content.
- Operative texts, to heed the extra-linguistic effect which the text is intended to achieve even if this has to be undertaken at the expense of both form and content.

In any case, what has long been another debate in Translation Studies is whether a classification of text types could be useful for translation. We could actually say that text typologies and establishing the aim of a translation is a really valuable tool to determine how appropriate or adequate a translation can be. Tasks under section 6.5. can be an example of different translations aims.

Nevertheless, when trying to cite a comprehensible typology of translations, maybe we could allude to Newmark (1981:12-15; 1989: 39-42) and establish the following taxonomy of text types in translation (extracted from Roberts 1995: 69-78):

> *a)* According to the *function of the SL text:*
> - translation of an expressive text, which focuses on the author and his style,
> - translation of an informative text, which emphasizes the content,
> - translation of a vocative text, where the focus is on the reader.
>
> *b)* According to the *style of the SL text:*
> - translation of narration,
> - translation of description,
> - translation of discussion,
> - translation of dialogue.
>
> *c)* According to the *content or subject matter of the SL text:*
> - scientific-technological translation,
> - institutional-cultural translation,
> - literary translation.
>
> *d)* According to the *general purpose of translating:*
> - translation for language teaching,
> - translation for professional purposes.
>
> *e)* According to the *translation approach used in producing the TL text:*
> - semantic translation, which attempts to render, as closely as the semantic and syntactic structures of the second language allow, the exact contextual meaning,
> - communicative translation, which attempts to produce on its readers an effect as close as possible to that obtained on the readers of the original.

6.2.3. Inverse translation

Most professional translators agree that translators are better when translating into their native language than into their foreign language though, under some circumstances, this situation can vary, as in the case of rare languages, field experts, bilinguals, etc. This assumption is clear if we take into account that no matter how proficient one is in the foreign language, inverse translation will always be more difficult than translating into one's native language, since the requirements are more demanding. As Jabak (2008) indicates, there are several reasons for this assumption:

- Only a native speaker of a language, being a good writer, will have the style, nuances and little subtleties which make a good translation. Being a good writer in our native language, by the way, is certainly important, since good writing skills are essential (excellent command of grammar and style).
- Translators have a more profound linguistic and cultural background of their native language than of a foreign language.
- The translator has a more natural and intuitive knowledge of the various linguistic elements of the native language, such as semantics, syntax, morphology and lexicology, etc. than the translator who translates into a foreign language.
- Translation into the native language enables translators to render cultural elements such as culturally bound terms, idioms, metaphors, collocations, and many others into adequate equivalents because they are born and bred in the culture into which they translate these cultural aspects or linguistic elements.

We should, however, be careful with the terms *inverse* or *indirect* translation, sometimes used as synonyms, as 'indirect' can be ambiguous and refer to several things:

- Translation from our mother tongue into a second or foreign language.
- Second hand or pivot translations of a ST, not directly from it, but via another translation.
- As opposed to direct translation, which corresponds to the idea that translation should convey the same meaning as the original, indirect translation involves looser degrees of resemblance.
- Back translation, or the process of translating a document that has already been translated into a foreign language back to the original language, preferably by an independent translator.

6.2.4. Translating culture

Translation inevitably involves two different languages and two different cultures, and the role of the translator is to mediate between those cultures. Many scholars agree with the fact that language is an expression of culture and individuality of its speakers and have, hence, deeply examined cultural-bound terms, or *realia*. Vlakhov and Florin (1970) seem to have been the first ones to coin the term *realia* to refer to cultural elements. The term has now been generalized and is frequently used to refer to such cultural words. As Cerdá Massó (1986: 248) states, it refers to objects, customs, habits, and other cultural and material aspects that have an impact in shaping a certain language. A good number of classifications and taxonomies for such cultural elements have thus been offered (Baker 1992, Katan 1999, Mayoral 1994, Molina 2001, Newmark 1988, Nida 1975, Santoyo 1994, Vlakhov y Florin 1970, etc.).

Following Nida (1975) and applying the concept of culture to the task of translation, Newmark (1988: 21) puts forth his classification of foreign cultural words, establishing five categories: (1) Ecology (flora, fauna, winds, climate, etc.); (2) material culture (food, clothes, houses, towns, transport); (3) social culture (work and leisure); (4) organizations, customs, activities, procedures or ideas, which include artistic, religious, political and administrative subcategories; and (5) gestures and habits.

Katan (1999) also provides a comprehensive view of how culture reveals itself at each of the following logical levels: (1) Environment (including climate, housing, food, etc.); (2) behaviour (actions and ways of behaving in certain cultures); (3) capabilities, strategies and skills used to communicate (including non-verbal communication, rituals, etc.); (4) values of the society and its hierarchy; (5) beliefs; and (6) identity.

Ku (2006: 91-98), reduces his taxonomy to the four generic types proposed by Molina (2001): (1) Environment: ecology, place names, etc.; (2) cultural heritage: religious beliefs, historical events, characters, festivities, folklore, housing, objects, etc.; (3) social culture: conventions, beliefs, habits, social organizations, etc.; and (4) linguistic culture: fixed expressions, idioms, insults, etc.

Finally, Fernández Guerra (2004) describes and exemplifies four major types of cultural referents which can turn translation into a very difficult process:

- Geographic and ethnographic terms, such *as albufera, gorrilla, Cockney*, or *The Square Mile*.

- Words or expressions referring to folklore, traditions and mythology. *Toro embolado, romería, peña, ...Ceilidh, Christmas stocking, touchdown, Tag* could exemplify them.

- Names of everyday objects, actions and events (such as food and drinks, clothes, housing, tools, public transport, dances and games, units of measurement, money, etc.): *Agua de Valencia, buñuelo, ... Christmas pudding, Bank holiday, cottage pie, Yorkshire pudding, happy hour, miles, earmuffs*, etc.

- Social and historical terms denoting territorial administrative units or divisions; departments, professions, titles, ranks, greetings and treatments; institutions, patriotic and religious organisations; etc.:

oposiciones, diputación provincial ... Sophomore, Salvation Army,
Christie's, YMCA, and so on and so forth.

Some authors such as Baker (1992: 21), Mayoral (1994: 76), Nord (1994),
Santoyo (1994: 143), and Marco Borillo (2002: 295-208) offer similar
classifications, emphasizing local colour, mannerisms, cultural and temporal
distance between two linguistic communities, etc. and recognising, more or less
explicitly, the difficulty, the inevitability of loss, or even impossibility of
translating these terms. And it is true that translating cultural elements, such as
the types mentioned above, cause many translation difficulties. But this does not
mean that they cannot be translated. In fact, along the lines of a good number of
theoreticians of translation, particularly those of the Leipzig school, all
languages can say (or are capable of saying) the same things; but, as a rule, all
of them say it in a different way. Indeed, should two languages say it in the
same way, then we would not be speaking of two languages, but of one and the
same language. The translator can indeed make recourse to several devices for
solving the problem of bridging the gap across cultures, provided that s/he is
culturally aware of those differences. S/he can rely on various procedures,
techniques or strategies to deal with such translation problems. The following
translations into Spanish of *Taste this Christmas pudding*, for example, could
illustrate it:

- Borrowing: Prueba este *Christmas pudding*.
- Adaptation: Prueba este turrón.
- Explanation: Prueba este dulce navideño hecho de frutas confitadas y coñac.
- Generalisation: Prueba este dulce.
- Literal translation: Prueba este pudín de Navidad.
- Reduction: Prueba esto.
- Etc.

The translator can coin or borrow the term from the SL into the TL, or
adapt it to suit the TC ('turrón' or 'roscón de Reyes'). It is also possible to
explain the conceptual differences in a footnote or in the text itself ('dulce
navideño hecho de frutas confitadas y coñac or pastel típico de Inglaterra'), and
so on. It is up to the translator to choose the most suitable way to render it in the
TL, and for the TC, depending on the aim, the time available, the potential
readers, etc. of his/her translation. In any case, the translator has to try to find
the most appropriate technique to convey cultural aspects in the TL place,
recognising the problems involved in translating some terms and taking into
account several options in order to provide the most appropriate solution for
each specific case. As regards how to approach the difficulties involved in

translating these terms, we are said to be faced with two main extremes: to transform the text so that it works under TC conditions, or to replace the source text functions with the respective meta-functions (Nord 2006: 59). This is actually an old issue in translation studies, which leads to the famous distinction between faithful or word-for-word translation and free or sense translation, already seen in previous sections of this book.

6.2.5. Translating literature

Most translations needed and done nowadays are non-literary translations. What seems amazing, nonetheless, is that most studies dealing with translation problems focus on literary translation. The reason is understandable if we take into account that form and content are equally important, literary texts are subject to different interpretations, transcend space and time, favour the exchange of cultures, revive old traditions, and contribute to the shaping of new literatures. It is indeed a difficult task, since the translator has to be able (1) to read, (2) to be a sort of critic and literary expert, and (3) to write as well as a writer. We could say that the main problems arising when translating literary text are due to (1) the message's form and content, (2) place and time differences between the readers of the SL and the TL, and (3) the translator's interpretation and way of translating.

When dealing with the translation of *prose*, some translators erroneously consider that there are no real problems, due to the widespread wrong belief that a novel or a similar literary text written in prose has simpler stylistic devices and a simpler structure than a poem, for instance, and can be translated in a straightforward way. But this is obviously not true, since a translator should try to convey, in the TL text, features such as any deviation from standard language (like dialectal forms, or regional linguistic devices particular to a specific region or social class), differences in time and place (either retaining the specificities of the original or modernising the translation), etc. Belloc proposed six general rules for the translator of prose texts (from Kumar 2008: 58-59):

- The translator should consider the work as an integral unit and translate in sections, asking himself what the whole sense is.
- The translator should render idiom by idiom.
- The translator must render intention by intention (the weight a given expression has in a particular context in the SL that would be different if translated literally into the TL).
- The translator should be careful with false friends.

- The essence of translating is 'the resurrection of an alien thing in a native body'.
- The translator should never embellish.

Dramatic texts also have their own specificities, since a dramatic text cannot be translated in the same way as a prose text. The main problem is that it is mainly written with dialogues that are to be interpreted in performance. As Bassnett's affirmative statement exclaims "a theatre text is read differently. It is read as something incomplete, rather than as a fully rounded unit, since it is only in performance that the full potential of the text is realised" (2014: 128-129). The translator should, thus, take into account the extralinguistic situation of the written text, features of the dialogue (like rhythm, intonation patterns, accent, loudness, …), sound effects, gestural text, undertext, scenery, etc. Consequently, the translator has two ways out:

- Performance-oriented translation, focusing mainly on playability or performability aspects, which could involve more freedom, fluency or a domesticating approach.
- Reader-oriented translation, translating the text as a purely literary text, focusing on readability and literalness, which could involve more fidelity or a foreignising method.

Of course, either way is followed, there can always be criticisms that either attack the translation as too literal and unperformable, or as too free and deviant from the original.

As regards the translation of *poetry*, Fernández Guerra (2012a) asks herself some questions, such as the following ones: how can one handle the formal elements of rhyme, meter and other prosodic devices? How can one play with words so as to transfer all the meanings involved in the SL text? Should one try to obtain a parallel form, at the expense of the content? Or rather the other way round? Should a translator of poetry be a poet as well? Or an expert on the SL poet? There will be always some 'loss'. Robert Frost, amongst others, was conscious of this when he tried to define poetry as "…that which is lost in translation". In any case, the difficulties involved in accounting for both content and form, sounds and associations, etc. can make us believe in the impossibility of poetical translation, which, in fact, has been often termed as "the art of the impossible". Similarly, Yifeng (2012: 231) indicates that "literary translation is primarily about translating the untranslatable or the seemingly untranslatable".

Nonetheless, a widely accepted classification of seven strategies to translate poetry is the one proposed by Lefevere (from Bassnett 2014: 93):

- Phonemic translation: to reproduce the SL sound in the TL (producing an acceptable paraphrase of the sentence, though the overall result can be clumsy and lack sense).
- Literal translation: emphasis on word-for-word translation (which destroys the sense and syntax of the original).
- Metrical translation: reproduction of the SL metre.
- Poetry into prose: converting a text into prose results on a distortion of the communicative value and syntax.
- Rhymed translation: in which the translator enters into a double restriction of metre and rhyme.
- Blank verse translation: again, there are restrictions imposed on the translator by the choice of structure.
- Interpretation: he mentions versions (the substance of the SL text is retained but the form is changed) and imitations (where the translator produces a poem of his own which has only a few things in common with the SL text).

And the eight stages proposed by Bly (1982: 68-89) when approaching the translation of a poem are also well known in the literature:

- Literal translation of the poem.
- See where that translation lost the meaning.
- Focus on the structure of the TL.
- Focus on how it sounds.
- Focus on the tone or mood of the poem (enthusiastic, melancholic, …).
- Focus on rhythm.
- Ask someone native (for further implications, tone, impression, …).
- Write a final draft, making final adjustments

Again, there can always be criticisms, no matter what approach we follow or how good or bad our translation can be, since there can be no one single right way of translating a poem, just as there is no single right way of writing one poem either.

6.3. How to translate well: duties and tips

Translation can sometimes be extremely difficult and we can face many practical problems, but it can also be a very rewarding and satisfying task, especially when we love languages. The translator should follow some requirements or responsibilities or abilities, according to the type of text to be translated, and the aim and audience of the translation, which will subsequently lead to some guidelines to follow:

- The translator should have a very good understanding and knowledge of the SL and SC. The tip here would be to try to analyse content, intention, linguistic and stylistic characteristics of language, translation problems, etc.

- The translator should have a perfect knowledge and be a skilled writer in the TL. We cannot, thus, assume that we will not make mistakes just because we are translating into our native language.

- The translator should practice and get experience in order to (1) re-express the text in the TL more easily, rapidly, accurately and appropriately; (2) choose the most adequate method; and (3) take into account timing (only use dictionaries when needed, for example).

- The translator should beware of machine translations. Sometimes it can be tempting to use a machine translation tool to save time, but it will invariably offer a bad translation and can make us miss the nuances of language. Of course, there are many electronic tools that can be useful (see section 7.2.), such as on-line dictionaries, for example, but we cannot rely on a total automatization of translation.

- The translator should be accurate and faithful to the SL text, so we should try to reproduce as exactly as possible the meaning and style of the SL text.

- The translator should look for naturalness in the TL, avoiding the tendency to translate word for word or very literally, and avoiding areas of interference (appropriateness of word order, verb tenses, collocations, …). Some translators try to listen to the words they write, reading their texts out loud to see if it sounds right.

- The translator should solve translation problems (register, cultural terms, stylistic devices, etc.). The advice could be to look for the most appropriate translation strategy (since everything is translatable into any language, in one way or another), and also to 'defend' any (in)conveniences of the translation against criticism.

- The translator should revise the TL text carefully, saving some time to read the translation, in order to correct spelling or punctuation mistakes, and to see if it is clearly written, if it makes sense, if it flows smoothly, etc. It can be useful to set it aside for a while and, after that hiatus, to read the translation again, without looking at the SL text (to avoid language interference), imagining that you are the end-user of the translation who is seeing it for the first time.

We could summarize these tips as follows:

Translation is not an easy and straightforward task, remember it.
Read the SL text carefully.
Analyse both content and form.
Naturalness in the translation and good writing skills are essential.
Skills and translation expertise are important, so practice as much as possible.
Language resources such as on-line dictionaries and tools can be very useful.
Accuracy and faithfulness to the SL text are very important.
Translation problems should be solved according to the aim of the translation.
Evaluate and revise the translation carefully.

6.4. Further readings

Bassnett, S. 2014. *Translation Studies*. New York: Routledge. [Chapter 3].
Bly, R. 1982. The Eight Stages of Translation. *The Kenyon Review*, Vol. 4: 68-89.
Jabak, O. 2008. Why is translation into the mother tongue more successful than into a second language? *Translation Directory*.
James, K. 2003. Cultural Implications for translation. *Translation Journal*, vol. 7, No. 1.
Roberts, R.P. 1995. Towards a typology of translations. *Hieronymus,* 1: 69-78.

6.5. Tasks

1. Some problems in English-Spanish translation are due to differences between both linguistic systems. Translate the following eight sentences (taken from Mott 2011: 71) into English, paying particular attention to word order (subject, verb, object, adverbs and adjuncts):

(a) En la redada policíaca fueron detenidas dos personas.

(b) Al formarse en este siglo las naciones actuales, los kurdos se quedaron sin territorio propio.

(c) Un carpintero en paro mató anoche en Granollers a una de sus hijas e hirió de gravedad a su mujer.

(d) Al poco tiempo de la llegada de Montse a la academia, se les unió en sus paseos postescolares otra chica, que se llamaba Nuria.

(e) La miseria y desamparo en que quedaron los soldados que participaron en la guerra ha generado un trauma de graves consecuencias.

(f) Aviones israelíes bombardearon ayer bases palestinas en las zonas próximas a la carretera que une Beirut con Damasco.

(g) De repente veo venir a lo lejos una persona. Aprieto con firmeza el bastón…

(h) Uno de los inconvenientes que tienen los bomberos es la escasa información que reciben las unidades de intervención.

2. Now translate the following eight sentences into Spanish, paying particular attention to the tense and form of the verbs (Mott 2011: 218):

(a) This is the first time I've visited this country.

(b) What a crook (that guy is)! This is the third time he's tried to swindle me!

(c) It can't have been very late when my aunt and uncle arrived and we sat down to dinner.

(d) His parents have not managed to convince him that he is very young to get married.

(e) I got a letter from the Town Hall this morning.

(f) The criminal had been suffering from severe depression for a long time.

(g) Sorry! I didn't realise you wanted to get by.

(h) Prices seem to be going up and up.

3. Text typology can present several problems for a translator. Have a look at the eight texts below and answer the following questions:

(a) In which contexts would we find those texts?

(b) Which is the main function in each? Which text type do you think they belong to?

(c) Which are the main lexical and structural differences between them?

(d) Which problems can the following texts pose for the translator?

(e) Do translators need to be thoroughly familiar with the subject matter or specialised language used?

(f) What skills are (or specific knowledge is) required of the translator in order to translate these texts?

(1) The FA Cup Final - Match Report

Manchester United completed their historic double Double by grinding out a win over the old enemy from the other end of the East Lancs Road. Liverpool had reached the Final with a flurry of goals, including one in each round from young England striker Robbie Fowler. But when it came to the big day, stars like Fowler failed to shine and the match didn't live up it to its billing as an "all-time classic."

After a bright but fruitless opening, United settled into a patient containing game to snuff out the threat from Liverpool's wild cards Steve McManaman and Stan Collymore. The ace in the pack was Roy Keane, commanding the midfield where John Barnes and Jamie Redknapp misfired. But despite the Irishman's sterling efforts, that man Cantona understandably stole the headlines with his glorious winner five minutes from the end. David James had been Liverpool's best player, making some quality saves from David Beckham and Eric Cantona, but he was caught out when Beckham swung in a late corner. The goalkeeper could only punch the ball downwards and it was deflected into Cantona's path. The Frenchman stepped back and volleyed home a piece of English football history. Can-tastique!

(2) Problem Page- Letters to Agony Aunt

Shy and afraid: I'm in love with a girl I know since two years ago. I don't know what to do to tell her what I feel. When I see her, I'm a nervous wreck. I'm afraid of making a tremendous bloomer. I'm also worried because I'm very shy and reserved, and she might turn me down. What shall I do?

Agony Aunt says...: Shy people are usually afraid of being afraid. They don't like other people knowing they are nervous and, when they try to hide it, it's even more difficult. You are probably a sensitive man that pushes away his feelings and who doesn't want to show them, since he is ashamed of them. You are very demanding and you are your own severest critic due to your own fears. There are two possible ways out: (1) A shy person is afraid of meeting new people, and might end up alone, without friends and without enjoying life. (2) He accepts his fears and his feelings, and behaves just as he is towards the rest. He risks more and more every time and he'll end up overcoming all the difficulties when he finds out that people love him. You have to learn how to fight your fears.

(3) NOD32 - New system upgrade! (environment version: 1.53)

New update and management system is among the most important changes implemented in this version. For detail information, please, visit us at: www.nod32.com.

New NOD32 Control Center module was integrated in NOD32. The Control Center was developed to support NOD32 multi-level network management and update system.

All NOD32 key modules are now equipped with automatic report messaging system. Virus incidents and other defined events can be sent via SMTP to any predefined address/es. Enhanced management of extensions of the files to be tested/scanned was implemented as well. New extensions can be added while the virus signature database is updated. No restart of the computer is required.

(4) Irish Porter Cake

Our porter cake is a special blend of Guinness Extra Stout, fruits and spices, matured carefully, giving a unique taste.

INGREDIENTS: SULTANAS (33%), WHEATFLOUR, FRESH EGGS, BROWN SUGAR, CAKE MARGARINE (PALM OIL, CANOLA OIL, HYDROGENATED PALM OIL), BUTTER, FRENCH GLANCE CHERRIES (6%), COLOURANT (3%), ORANGE AND LEMON PEEL (3%), NATURAL LEMON FLAVOUR, GLYCERINE, MIXED SPICE, SALT, GUINNESS EXTRA STOUT, (4.7%) (0.018% ALC.VOL.) PRODUCT OF IRELAND   NET WEIGHT 444G E 14OZ STORE IN A COOL PLACE

(5) Tributación de no residentes: Personas físicas

CONSIDERACIONES: DERECHO INTERNO ESPAÑOL

La forma en que una persona física debe tributar en España se determina en función de si la misma es o no residente en este país.

Según la ley española una persona es RESIDENTE FISCAL en territorio español cuando se dé cualquiera de las siguientes circunstancias:

- que permanezca más de 183 días, durante el año natural, en territorio español, o
- que radique en España el núcleo principal o la base de sus actividades empresariales o profesionales o de sus intereses económicos.

Para determinar el período de permanencia en territorio español se computarán sus ausencias temporales, salvo que demuestre su residencia habitual en otro país durante 183 días en el año natural.

Asimismo, se presumirá, salvo prueba en contrario, que una persona tiene su residencia habitual en territorio español, cuando residan habitualmente en España el cónyuge no separado legalmente y los hijos menores de edad que dependan de aquél.

(6) Welcome to the Metropolitan Museum of Art.

The Metropolitan Museum of Art is one of the largest and finest art museums in the world. Its collections include more than two million works of art —several hundred thousands of which are on view at any given time— spanning more than 5,000 years of world culture, from prehistory to the present.

This brochure is designed to give visitors an overview of the collections on display in the Museum's galleries. Also available are a Floor Plan, which includes information on services for visitors, and the Calendar, which offers a detailed current listing of special exhibitions, concerts, lectures, films, and other Museum activities. *The Metropolitan Museum of Art Guide,* an illustrated handbook that is for sale in all of the Museum's shops, provides more information about the collections.

The Metropolitan Museum was founded in 1870 by a group of distinguished public figures, philanthropists, and artists. It moved to its site in Central Park in 1880. The Beaux-Arts facade and Great Hall were designed by the American architect Richard Morris Hunt at the turn of the century, and the Museum has grown considerably since then. It now extends along Fifth Avenue from 80th to 84th streets. Art is displayed on two main floors and in additional gallery areas. The collections are divided into eighteen curatorial departments, described below, which are responsible for the acquisition, preservation, and exhibition of the works of art.

(7) Anna Hotel - London

60 ENSUITE ROOMS

WITH MODERN FACILITIES

BAR COFFEE SHOP

ROOM SERVICE

MEETING & CONFERENCE

ROOM AVAILABLE

IDEAL FOR THE

BUSINESSMAN

SECRETARIAL SERVICES

AVAILABLE

ALL MAJOR CREDIT CARDS

ACCEPTED

NEXT TO HYDE PARK. TWO BLOCKS FROM
QUESSNSWAY & BAYSWATER UNDERGROUND STATIONS
FAST & EASY ACCESS TO THE CITY, EARLS COURT & OLYMPIA
HEATHROW AIRBUS STOPS NEARBY

0171 221 6622
FAX 0171 792 9656

(8) The Big Bang Theory - Series 3 - Episode 09

Howard:	So two years later, there's a knock on the door, guy opens it, and there on his porch is the snail, who says, "What the heck was all that about?"
Bernadette:	I don't really get it.
Howard:	Well, see, it took two years for the snail to... *(she kisses him)* not important.
Bernadette:	Can I ask you a question?
Howard:	Sure.
Bernadette:	Where do you think this is going?
Howard:	To be honest, I was hoping at least second base.
Bernadette:	You're so funny. You're like a stand-up comedian.
Howard:	A Jewish stand-up comedian, that'd be new.
Bernadette:	Actually, I think a lot of them are Jewish.
Howard:	No, I was just... never mind.
Bernadette:	Look, Howard, this is our third date and we both know what that means.
Howard:	We do?
Bernadette:	Sex.
Howard:	You're kidding.
Bernadette:	But I need to know whether you're looking for a relationship or a one-night stand.
Howard:	Okay, just to be clear, there's only one correct answer, right? It's not like chicken or fish on an airplane?
Bernadette:	Maybe you need to think about it a little.
Howard:	You know, it's not unheard of for a one-night stand to turn into a relationship.
Bernadette:	Call me when you figure it out.
Howard:	Three dates means sex? Who knew?

Scene: The apartment.

Howard:	Greetings, homies, homette.
Penny:	Why are you back from your date so early?
Howard:	In romance, as in show business, always leave them wanting more.
Penny:	What exactly does that mean?
Leonard:	He struck out.

4. Have a look at the following text on *Philology*. Can you think of any problems for English-Spanish translation?

Words in the Mind

This book deals with words. It sets out to answer the questions: how do humans manage to store so many words, and how do they find the ones they want? In brief, it discusses the nature of the human word-store, or 'mental lexicon'. This is a topic which has recently attracted the attention of a large number of researchers. Unfortunately, most of the work is tucked away in scholarly journals and conference proceedings. It is also excessively fragmented, since many of those working on the subject have concerned themselves only with a small section of it. This book is an attempt to make recent findings on the mental lexicon available to a wide range of people, and to provide a coherent overall picture of the way it might work. Hopefully, it will prove of interest to anyone concerned with words: students of linguistics and psychology, speech therapists, language teachers, educationalists, lexicographers, and the general reader who would just like to know how humans remember words and how children learn them. It could also be regarded as a general introduction to linguistics from a novel angle. I am grateful to friends and colleagues who made a number of useful comments and valuable suggestions on various chunks of the book or reported slips of the tongue which I have included in it. And finally, a stylistic point. I have used two devices to combat the sexism which is widespread in the English language. In some places, I have used *she* as well as *he* when a neutral between-sexes pronoun is required. In other places, I have followed the increasingly common practice of using *they* and *their* as singular forms after a neutral noun.

[J. Aitchison 1993]

5. University newspapers can always provide us with texts that can be difficult to translate. For example, translate one of the following texts into Spanish, trying to retain all the factic information present in the original:

(a) Cheating Oxford President expelled

The President of Oxford University Student Union has been expelled after being discovered to have cheated in her finals.
Katherine Rainwood, 22, is said to being likely to appeal against the decision to expel her, despite apparently pleading guilty at the original hearing. A spokeswoman for the prestigious University said: "I can confirm Katherine Rainwood was found to have used unfair means in her exams following an investigation by the Proctors. She was sent down."

Reports in the national newspapers have indicated that Ms Rainwood cheated by downloading an essay which she had written prior to her exam. She was sitting the exam in a separate room and with the use of a computer after telling the University she had injured her wrist.

Ms Rainwood has been unavailable for comment, and her father has said that she is currently in Germany. The Politics, Philosophy and Economics student had resigned as President just two days after taking up the post. Her resignation statement failed to mention the exam scandal, instead citing personal reasons as the cause of her inability to continue as President. The statement read: "Due to extremely difficult personal circumstances with great sadness that I resign my position of President, with immediate effect. This is one of the hardest decisions in my life to make, and I am very upset to be leaving Oxford and OUSU (Oxford University Student Union). I apologise greatly for having to let you down at this point."

Acting President, Mark Strathdene, responded to the news by saying: "This is a complete surprise. We knew she had resigned but had no idea why." The official Union response states: "We regret her resignation and wish her luck for the future."

Ms Rainwood, who had studied at the all female St. Hilda's College, had been elected on a ticket of "Labour students against top-up fees". A spokesman for the Labour Party commented: "Ms Rainwood is no longer a member of Labour Students. We understand she resigned the Presidency of the Student's Union for personal reasons."

Ms Rainwood's former headmistress described her as a brilliant scholar, saying that it would have been totally out of character for her former pupil to cheat. One relative described her as: "a very bright girl; she doesn't need to cheat."   [Jon Arnold]

(b) Drinking to Oblivion?

Do you know how much you drink? Probably more than you think. What about all those drinks you threw down your neck at Pop Tarts? The quick pint between lectures? The wine you had with a meal?

Try to total the alcoholic units you drank in the past week. Scared? Or is your short term memory gone to the point where you can't remember?

Last week the Welfare Committee attempted to get us all to remember. Alcohol Awareness Week was about "trying to get us all to at least drink sensibly," says Lindsay Pinkerton, a Welfare Committee member, "if someone picks up a leaflet in Bar One, then they'll know a bit more about it, and hopefully think about what they're doing to their body the next time they go out."

Although you can say people do think about what they are doing. They think about it when they're hung over, when they are cringing at last night's dodgy pull and when their stomach muscles finally give up. Rarely does anyone consider what a major bender could do to their liver, to their brain. Cirrhosis and depression last a bit longer than a morning's embarrassment and nausea. But it doesn't stop anyone going out for a quick one, does it?

"Well what can you say?" comments Economics student David o'Neil, gesturing at Bar One.

"Something like Alcohol Awareness probably isn't going to cut down the amounts students drink, not as long as there are offers like this, a pint for a pound." says Andy McFarlane, a Journalism student.

Drinking is something you do at university. It's part of the student stereotype, like smoking, casual sex and watching Richard and Judy. You'll be much healthier when you graduate, honest.

The morning-after promises to never drink anything, ever again, ever, don't usually come to much. Drinking is an integral part of university life, even if the Union does serve non-alcoholic cocktails now.

For some people though, drinking is more than a silly night on the piss.

"I went to university, and I failed miserably at it," says a member of Alcoholics Anonymous. "I felt like a square peg in a round hole. With a drink I felt comfortable, I drank more and more.

"It became an intractable situation, I could not get through a day without drinking. You've heard of Dutch courage, I needed Dutch courage to live for a day."

One more before last orders is fun, relaxing, a laugh with mates. Alcohol isn't an addiction for everybody, but as the AA member said, "I thought I was in control, but really it was in control of me."

6. Inverse translation: Read these fragments and suggest suitable translations into English for all the phrases that are in italics. Be careful with idioms, sayings, proverbs, puns, etc. You will have to translate problems such as linguistic or cultural untranslatability through various mechanisms, such as compensation, loans, explanatory notes, adaptation, equivalence, paraphrasing, analogies, etc.

La romería

La romería era muy tradicional; la gente se *hacía lenguas* de lo bien que se pasaba en la romería, adonde llegaban todos los años visitantes de muchas leguas a la redonda.

Unos venían a caballo y otros en unos autobuses adornados con ramas; pero lo realmente típico era ir en carro de bueyes; a los bueyes les pintaban los cuernos con *albayalde* o *blanco de España* y les adornaban la testuz con margaritas y amapolas...

El cabeza de familia vino todo el tiempo pensando en la romería; en el tren, la gente no hablaba de otra cosa.

– *¿Te acuerdas cuando Paquito, el de la de Telégrafos, le saltó el ojo a la doña Pura?*

– Sí que me acuerdo; aquella sí que *fue sonada*. Un guardia civil decía que tenía que venir el señor juez a levantar el ojo.

– *¿Y te acuerdas de cuando aquel señorito se cayó, con pantalón blanco y todo, en la sartén del churrero?*

– También me acuerdo. ¡Qué voces pegaba el condenado! *¡En seguida se echaba de ver que eso de estar frito debe dar mucha rabia!*

[...]

El cabeza de familia estaba encantado de ver lo bien que había caído su proyecto de ir todos juntos *a merendar* a la romería.

Levantaron a los niños media hora antes, les dieron el desayuno y *los prepararon de domingo*; hubo sus prisas y sus carreras, porque media hora es tiempo que pronto pasa, pero al final se llegó a tiempo.

[...]

Al padre se le ocurrió que diesen todos juntos, con él a la cabeza, un paseíto por unos desmontes que había detrás de la casa, pero la madre dijo que *eso no se le hubiera ocurrido ni al que asó la manteca*, y que los niños lo que necesitaban era estar descansados para por la tarde.

[...]

Los niños, que no se hacían cargo de las cosas, se portaron muy mal y *se pusieron perdidos de tierra*; de todos ellos, la única que se portó un poco bien fue Encarnita – que llevaba un trajecito azulina y un gran lazo malva en el pelo –, pero la pobre tuvo mala suerte, porque le picó una avispa en un carrillo, y doña Adela, su abuelita, que la oyó gritar, *salió hecha un basilisco*, la llamó mañosa y antojadiza y le dio media docena de tortas, dos de ellas bastante fuertes.

Después, cuando doña Adela se dio cuenta de que a la nieta lo que le pasaba era que le había picado una avispa, le empezó a hacer arrumacos y a compadecerla, y se pasó el resto de la mañana apretándole *una perra gorda* contra la picadura.

[...]

La comida tardó algo más que de costumbre, porque con eso de haber madrugado tanto, ya se sabe: *la gente se confía y, al final, los unos por los otros, la casa sin barrer.*

A eso de las tres o tres y cuarto, el cabeza de familia y los suyos se sentaron a la mesa.

Tomaron de primer plato fabada asturiana; al cabeza de familia, en verano, le gustaban mucho las ensaladas y los gazpachos y, en general, los platos en crudo.

Después tomaron filetes, y de postre, un plátano. A la niña de la avispa le dieron, además, un caramelo de menta; el angelito tenía el carrillo como un volcán.

Su padre, para consolarla, le explicó que peor había quedado la avispa, insecto que se caracteriza, entre otras cosas, porque, para herir, sacrifica su vida.

La niña decía «¿Sí? », pero *no tenía un gran aire de estar oyendo eso que se llama una verdad como una casa,* ni denotaba, tampoco, un interés excesivo, digámoslo así.   [C.J. Cela]

7. As you have probably noticed by now, translating 'culture' can be a real problem for a translator, since some texts are so culture-bound that it's quite hard to achieve a balance between fluency and fidelity. Analyse and translate the following text dealing with the Spanish tradition of *Tapas*:

Tapas

La liturgia del tapeo es un viejo y nutritivo ritual que tiene su origen en Sevilla. En un principio se redujo a generosas lonchas de embutido que 'tapaban' el recipiente que el vino contenía, de ahí el nombre de 'tapa'. Pero el tapeo tal cual hoy se considera toma carta de naturaleza cuando incorpora a su nómina guisos y fritos de cocina, servidos en pequeñas porciones. De tal forma que el tapeo, o tapiñeo, no deja de ser una forma de comer en cómodos plazos. Hasta el punto de que en Andalucía existe la placentera costumbre, que ya se ha extendido por toda España, de 'ir a comer de tapas'. Costumbre que incluso ha llegado a ese lejano pueblo que lleva el extraño nombre de 'Allende Nuestras Fronteras'.

Hagamos una sencilla consideración aritmético-gastronómica: el peso medio de una tapa, según la sevillana ortodoxia, es de setenta gramos. A partir de los cien gramos, la tapa adquiere rango de 'ración', y eso es ya otro cantar. Bien, la dieta alimenticia de una persona normal, en un almuerzo normal, es de cuatrocientos gramos. Es decir, que cualquier persona normal que gratifique su estómago en seis cómodos plazos tapeantes puede decirse que ha almorzado. Un menú sevillanísimo podría ser este: salpicón de marisco, ensaladilla rusa, pavía de bacalao, espinacas con garbanzos, calamares fritos y cola de toro. Todo un festín. Claro que hay personas insaciables que tapean sin son ni medida. Tengo yo una amiga, gorda ella por razones obvias, que cuando va por la tapa número dieciséis comenta tan tranquila: 'Ya no quiero ninguna tapa más, porque luego llego a casa y no como'. Hace falta tener poca vergüenza.

Conviene señalar que el tapeo como Dios manda, el tapeo secundum Sevilla, que es su cuna, está sujeto a algunos preceptos que no todos los practicantes cumplen. El tapeo clásico no es sedente; es itinerante, es peripatético. Cierto que cada cual es muy dueño de saborear sus bocados en la posición que más se le antoje, pero cierto es también que el buen tapeante desdeña la mesa o velador y prefiere la práctica del condumio a pie de mostrador. Y que jamás prueba más de dos tapas en un mismo lugar. El tapeo lo reparte a lo largo de distintos bares, tascas o tabernáculos, por lo general cercanos unos a otros, con lo cual se cumple el precepto de la peripeteia manducante. Otro detalle digno de considerar es la forma, según sevillana costumbre, en que los bares informan a su parroquia de la nómina del sólido suministro. La lista de tapas suele figurar escrita en pizarras o en carteles con mensaje publicitario al pie, colgados en la pared posterior a la barra. Pero aún subsiste, cada vez menos desgraciadamente, la vieja costumbre del tapeo recitado, de la transmisión de la oferta por vía oral. Y aún quedan auténticos expertos en la prédica gastronómica, eximios divos del recitativo culinario. Hace poco tiempo falleció uno de los grandes maestros de arte tan singular: Quico, el dueño del bar que su nombre lleva, situado en el popular barrio de Triana. Su personalísima letanía incluía nada menos que sesenta tapas distintas. La mayor parte del público que al bar acudía lo hacía más para escuchar que para comer. Era mucha la gente que se alimentaba 'comiendo de oído'. Tras la audición de la sabrosa salmodia, que el solista repetía mil y una veces al día, el personal elegía cualquiera de las tapas por puro trámite. Los miércoles de cada semana el bar Quico permanecía cerrado. Y un letrero en la puerta advertía, en lugar de 'Cerrado por descanso del personal', 'Cerrado por descanso de la lengua'. Lógico.

8. Now analyse and translate the following text, in which culture is also so present... You will find sentences which could be misunderstood or easily mistranslated. Some of them could even be called *untranslatable*, due to some vocabulary items and cultural references. Suggest how they could be rendered in English.

Los Sanfermines. De ¡Viva San Fermín! a ¡Pobre de mí!

ILUSIÓN. Las 204 horas que transcurren entre el chupinazo del 6 de julio y el 'Pobre de mí' del 14 no son suficientes para los más sanfermineros. De ahí que muchos pamploneses, al ritmo de 'Uno de enero, dos de febrero' inicien el primer día del año una peculiar e ilusionante escalera, ocurrente excusa para juntarse en torno a una mesa, darle un repaso a las fiestas del año anterior y, sobre todo, ir preparando las próximas.

EMOCIÓN. Los sanfermines son fiestas de emociones. Claro que poner negro sobre blanco esa faceta de nuestras vidas no deja de ser un reto complicado. Me limitaré a comentar que muchos la viven el 6 de julio, cuando el chupinazo asciende por encima de la Casa Consistorial anunciando el inicio de la fiesta. Otros tienden a emocionarse al paso de la procesión de San Fermín, mientras algún txistulari o jotero dedica alguna pieza al santo. El encierro, por supuesto, también pone frecuentemente la piel de gallina. En San Fermín, creo haberlo dicho, las emociones encuentran fácil acomodo. Y algunas son tan fuertes que nunca se olvidan.

MÚSICA. Sin música no habría sanfermines y sin Manuel Turrillas alguien tendría que inventarla de nuevo. El popular músico, de cuyo nacimiento se cumplen cien años, es el creador de la clásica estampa sanferminera, mezcla de biribilketa y jota, que utilizó para escribir los himnos a las peñas de la ciudad. Turrillas fue clarinetista de La Pamplonesa, la banda municipal (qué lujo de banda!) presente en todos los momentos clave de la fiesta. En sanfermines también suenan el txistu, la gaita, las fanfarres y multitud de grupos, de todo tipo y calidad, que recorren las calles del casco viejo arrastrando tras de sí a la gente y formando un continuo y variado concierto.

GRANDEZA. La grandeza de los gigantes, tan grandes que son capaces de devolvernos todos los años a la infancia. Se los debemos a Tadeo Amorena, artesano nacido en el precioso barrio Bozate de Arizkun, mítico enclave de la marginada raza de los agotes. Son cuatro parejas de reyes y reinas que representan a un mundo al que le falta Oceanía y cuentan con una pintoresca corte de kilikis, cabezudos y zaldikos que les preceden. En las mañanas sanfermineras, nada como perderse por las estrechas calles medievales de la ciudad y estar atento al sonido de la gaita. Después aparecerán niños huyendo de los kilikis. Y detrás, majestuosas, las figuras de los gigantes de Pamplona con su casi siglo y medio tan bien llevado. Lo dejó escrito Friaco Iraizoz, un popular poeta pamplonés del siglo XIX: '¿Oyes las notas vibrantes de esa gaita tan chillona? / Pues espera unos instantes / que vas a ver a los gigantes / los gigantes de Pamplona'.

DESMADRE. Es componente fundamental de estas fiestas. En San Fermín se hacen cosas que nadie en su sano juicio firmaría, como ponerse delante de un toro de seiscientos kilos, bailar hasta reventar, acudir diariamente a la corrida sin ser aficionado, o comer y beber como si fuera a acabarse el mundo. Claro que algunos traspasan la barrera del desmadre para instalarse en la imbecilidad cuando agarran a los toros en el encierro, dan suelta a sus ganas de bronca o se tiran de lo alto de una fuente confiando en que alguien les recogerá antes de estrellarse contra el adoquín de la calle Navarrería. Debe ser el tributo, generosamente pagado, por tener unas fiestas tan famosas.

PENA. No sé si será por la ilusión, el santo, el toro, la emoción, la música, la grandeza o el desmadre de los sanfermines, seguramente por todo eso y por otras muchas razones, pero la cuestión es que llega el día 14 y uno comprueba, apenado, que el paso del tiempo es inexorable, también durante este fantástico paréntesis. La letra de la última canción de fiestas lo resume así de bien: 'Pobre de mí, pobre de mí, se han acabado las fiestas de San Fermín'.

9. In extracts from literary texts we can also find all sorts of problems for the translator. For instance, why can the following factors affect literary translation?

   (a) Place & time

   (b) Form & content

   (c) Translator's interpretation & way of translating

10. Translate the following passage into Spanish and identify all translation strategies you have used.

Brooklyn

An abandoned church, a For Rent sign defacing its baroque facade, towers black and broken at the corner of this lost square; sparrows nest among the stone flowers carved above its chalked up door (Kilroy was here, Seymour loves Betty, You Stink!); inside, where sunlight falls on shattered pews, all manner of stray beasts have found a home: one sees misty cats watching from its windows, hears queer animal cries, and neighborhood children, who dare each other to enter there, come forth toting bones they claim as human (yeah, they is so! I'm tellin' yuh; the guy was kilt). Definitive in its ugliness, the church for me symbolizes some elements of Brooklyn: if a similar structure were destroyed, I have the uneasy premonition that another, equally old and monstruous, would swiftily be erected, for Brooklyn, or the chain of cities so-called, has, unlike Manhattan, no interest in architectural change. Nor it is lenient toward the individual: in despair one views the quite endless stretches of look-alike bungalows, ginger-bread and brownstones, the inevitable empty, ashy lot where the sad, sweet, violent children, gathering leaves and tenement-wood, make October bonfires, the sad, sweet children chasing down those glassy August streets to Kill the Kike! Kill the Wop! Kill the Dinge! -a custom of this country where the mental architecture, like the houses, is changeless.

Manhattan friends, unwilling to cope with the elaborately dismal subway trip (Oh B, do come, I swear to you it takes only forty minutes, and honest you don't have to change trains but three times) say so-sorry to any invitation. For this reason I've often day-dreamed of leasing and renovating the church: who could resist visiting so curious a residence? As matters stand I have two rooms in a brown-stone duplicated by twenty others on the square; the interior of the house is a grimy jungle of Victoriana: lily-pale, plump-faced ladies garbed in rotting Grecian veils prance tribally on wallpaper; in the hall an empty, tarnished bowl for calling cards, and a hat-tree, gnarled like a spruce glimpsed on the coast of Brittany, are elegant mementos from Brooklyn's less blighted days; the parlor bulges with dusty fringed furniture, a family history in daguerreotype parades across an old untuned piano, everywhere antimacassars are like little crocheted flags declaring a state of Respectability, and when a draught goes through this room beaded lamps tinkle Oriental tunes.

However, there are telephones: two upstairs, three down and 125 in the basement; for it is in the basement that my landladies are more or less locked to a switchboard: Mrs. Q., a waddling, stunted woman with a red bulldog face, knobby lavender eyes, and bright orange, unbelievable hair which, like her daughter Miss Q., she wears wild and waist-length, is a suspicious person, and her suspicion is the sort that goes with those who, despising everything, are looking for a reason. Poor Miss Q. is simply tired; soft and honeyed, she labors under what is essentially a birth-to-death fatigue, and at times I wonder whether she is really Miss Q. or Zasu Pitts. [Truman Capote]

11. Read the passage below, identify any deviation from standard language. Should we translate this using a Spanish dialect or any features in Spanish that deviate from the standard?

The Adventures of Huckleberry Finn

'Well, I did. I said I wouldn't, and I'll stick to it. Honest *injun* I will. People would call me a low down Ablitionist and despise me for keeping mum- but that don't make no difference. I ain't agoing to tell, and I ain't agoing back there anyways. So now, le's know all about it.'

'Well, you see, it 'uz dis way. Ole Missus - dat's Miss Watson - she pecks on me all de time, en treats me pooty rough, but she awluz said she wouldn' sell me down to Orleans. But I noticed dey wuz a nigger trader roun' de place considable, lately, en I begin to git oneasy. Well, one night I creeps to de do', pooty late, en de do' warn't quite shet, en I hear ale missus tell de widder she gwyne to sell me down to Orleans, but she didn'

want ta, but she could git eight hund'd dollars for me, en it 'uz sich a big
stack o' money she couldn' resis'. De widder she try to git her to say she
wouldn' do it, but I never waited to hear the res'. I lit out mighty quick, I
tell you.   [Mark Twain]

12. Translate this short passage into Spanish. How can factors such as time and
    place affect the target language text? You can either retain the specificities
    of the original, capturing the flavour of the past (*historicising* translation),
    or create an air of contemporary relevance (*modernising* translation):

The Longest Journey

Sawston School had been founded by a tradesman in the seventeenth
century. It was then a tiny grammar-school in a tiny town, and the City
Company who governed it had to drive half a day through the woods and
heath on the occasion of their annual visit. In the twentieth century they
still drove, but only from the railway station; and found themselves not in
a tiny town, nor yet in a large one, but amongst innumerable residences,
detached and semi-detached, which had gathered round the school. For
the intentions of the founder had been altered, or at all events amplified,
instead of educating the "poor of my home", he now educated the upper
classes of England. The change had taken place not so very far back. Till
the nineteenth century the grammar-school was still composed of day
scholars from the neighbourhood. Then two things happened. Firstly, the
school's property rose in value, and it became rich. Secondly, for no
obvious reason, it suddenly emitted a quantity of bishops. The bishops,
like the stars from a Roman candle, were all colours, and flew in all
directions, some high, some low, some to distant colonies, one into the
Church of Rome. But many a father traced their course in the papers;
many a mother wondered whether her son, if properly ignited, might not
burn as bright; many a family moved to the place where living and
education were so cheap, where day-boys were not looked down upon,
and where the orthodox and the up-to-date were said to be combined. The
school doubled its numbers. It built new class-rooms, laboratories and
gymnasium. It dropped the prefix "Grammar". It coaxed the sons of the
local tradesmen into a new foundation, the "Commercial School", built a
couple of miles away. And it started boarding-houses. It had not the
gracious antiquity of Eton or Winchester, nor, on the other hand, had it a
conscious policy like Lancing, Wellington, and other purely modern
foundations. Where traditions served, it clung to them. Where new
departures seemed desirable, they were made. It aimed at producing the
average Englishman, and, to a very great extent, it succeeded.

                                                                     [E.M. Forster]

13. Consider the problems which arise when we translate the following extract from the point of view of register. What extra problems does the sort of language used in this text raise for translators?

Red Harvest

The man who stood there was a stranger to me. He was young, thin and gaudily dressed. He had heavy eyebrows and a small moustache that were coal-black against a very pale, nervous but not timid, face.

'I'm Ted Wright', he said, holding out a hand as if I were glad to meet him. 'I guess you've heard Whisper talk about me.'

I gave him my hand, let him in, closed the door, and asked: 'You're a friend of Whisper's?'

'You bet'. He held up two thin fingers pressed tightly together. 'Just like that, me and him'.

I didn't say anything. He looked around the room, smiled nervously, crossed to the open bathroom door, peeped in, came back to me, rubbed his lips with his tongue, and made his proposition:

'I'll knock him off for you for half a grand.'

'Whisper?'

'Yep, and it's dirt cheap.'

'Why do I want him killed?' I asked.

'He un-womaned you, didn't he?'

'Yeah?'

'You ain't that dumb.'

A notion stirred in my noodle. To give it time to crawl around I said: 'Sit down. This needs talking over.'

'It don't need nothing,' he said, looking at me sharply, not moving towards either chair. 'You either want him knocked off or you don't.'

'Then I don't.'

He said something I didn't catch, down in his throat, and turned to the door. I got between him and it. He stopped, his eye fidgeting.

I said: 'So Whisper's dead?'

He stepped back and put a hand behind him. I poked his jaw, leaning my hundred and ninety pounds on the poke.

He got his legs crossed and went down.

I pulled him up by the wrists, yanked his face close to mine, and growled:

'Come through. What's the racket?'

'I ain't done nothing to you.'

'Let me catch you. Who got Whisper?'

'I don't know nothing a –'

I let go one of his wrists, slapped his face with my open hand, caught his wrist again, and tried my luck at crunching both of them while I repeated:

'Who got Whisper?'

'Dan Rolff,' he whined. 'He walked up to him and stuck him with the same skewer Whisper had used on the twist. That's right.'

'How do you know it was the one Whisper killed the girl with?'

'Dan said so.'

'What did Whisper say?'

'Nothing. He looked funny as hell, standing there with the butt of the sticker sticking out his side. Then he flashes the rod and puts two pills in Dan just like one, and the both of them go down together, cracking heads, Dan's all bloody through the bandages.'

'And then, what?'

'Then nothing. I roll them over, and they are a pair of stiffs. Every word I'm telling you is gospel.'

'Who else was there?'

'Nobody else. Whisper was hiding out, with only me to go between him and the mob. He killed Noonan hisself, and he didn't want to have to trust nobody for a couple of days, till he could see what was what, excepting me.'

'So you, being a smart boy, thought you could run around to his enemies and pick up a little dough for killing him after he was dead?'

'I was clean, and this won't be no place for Whisper's pals when the word gets out that he's croaked,' Wright whined. 'I had to raise a get-away stake.'   [D. Hammett]

14. Browse through the text below and confront potential translation difficulties in the text with suitable translation procedures. Then translate a portion of the text and discuss the (in)convenience of the translation you propose.

The Gold Bug

                                                        -- *All in the Wrong*

Many years ago, I contracted an intimacy with a Mr. William Legrand. He was of an ancient Huguenot family, and had once been wealthy; but a series of misfortunes had reduced him to want. To avoid the mortification consequent upon his disasters, he left New Orleans, the city of his forefathers, and took up his residence at Sullivan's Island, near Charleston, South Carolina.

                                        [...]

In the inmost recesses of this coppice, not far from the eastern or more remote end of the island, Legrand had built himself a small hut, which he occupied when I first, by mere accident, made his acquaintance. This soon ripened into friendship -- for there was much in the recluse to excite interest and esteem. I found him well educated, with unusual powers of mind, but infected with misanthropy, and subject to perverse moods of alternate enthusiasm and melancholy. He had with him many books, but rarely employed them. His chief amusements were gunning and fishing, or sauntering along the beach and through the myrtles, in quest of shells or entomological specimens -- his collection of the latter might have been envied by a Swammerdamm. In these excursions he was usually accompanied by an old negro, called Jupiter, who had been manumitted before the reverses of the family, but who could be induced, neither by threats nor by promises, to abandon what he considered his right of attendance upon the footsteps of his young "Massa Will." It is not improbable that the relatives of Legrand, conceiving him to be somewhat unsettled in intellect, had contrived to instil this obstinacy into Jupiter, with a view to the supervision and guardianship of the wanderer.

Just before sunset I scrambled my way through the evergreens to the hut of my friend, whom I had not visited for several weeks. Upon reaching the hut I rapped, as was my custom, and getting no reply, sought for the key where I knew it was secreted, unlocked the door, and went in. I threw off an overcoat, took an arm-chair by the crackling logs, and awaited patiently the arrival of my hosts.

Soon after dark they arrived, and gave me a most cordial welcome. Jupiter, grinning from ear to ear, bustled about to prepare some marsh-hens for supper. Legrand was in one of his fits -- how else shall I term them? -- of enthusiasm. He had found an unknown bivalve, forming a new genus, and, more than this, he had hunted down and secured, with Jupiter's assistance, a *scarabæus* which he believed to be totally new, but in respect to which he wished to have my opinion on the morrow.

"And why not to-night?" I asked, rubbing my hands over the blaze, and wishing the whole tribe of *scarabæi* at the devil.

"Ah, if I had only known you were here!" said Legrand, "but it's so long since I saw you; and how could I foresee that you would pay me a visit this very night of all others? As I was coming home I met Lieutenant G-- - - , from the fort, and, very foolishly, I lent him the bug; so it will be impossible for you to see it until the morning. Stay here to-night, and I will send Jup down for it at sunrise. It is the loveliest thing in creation!"

"What? -- sunrise?"

"Nonsense! no! -- the bug. It is of a brilliant gold color -- about the size of a large hickory-nut -- with two jet black spots near one extremity of the back, and another, somewhat longer, at the other. The *antennæ* are-- "

"Dey aint *no* tin in him, Massa Will, I keep a tellin' on you," here interrupted Jupiter; "de bug is a goole-bug, solid, ebery bit of him, inside and all, sep him wing -- meber feel half so hebby a bug in my life."

[E. A. Poe]

15. Translate this scene from a theatre text. Your translation should be either (1)
    performance-oriented, so you are faced with the criterion of *playability* as
    a pre-requisite, or (2) reader-oriented, as a *purely literary* text. Don't forget
    the title!

The Importance of Being Earnest

ALGERNON. Did you hear what I was playing, Lane?

LANE. I didn't think it polite to listen, sir.

ALGERNON. I'm sorry for that, for your sake. I don't play accurately - any one
can play accurately - but I play with wonderful expression. As far as
the piano is concerned, sentiment is my forte. I keep science for
Life.

LANE. Yes, sir.

ALGERNON. And, speaking of the science of Life, have you got the cucumber
sandwiches cut for Lady Bracknell?

LANE. Yes, sir. [Hands them on a salver.]

ALGERNON. [Inspects them, takes two, and sits down on the sofa.] Oh! ... by the
way, Lane, I see from your book that on Thursday night, when Lord
Shoreman and Mr. Worthing were dining with me, eight bottles of
champagne are entered as having been consumed.

LANE. Yes, sir; eight bottles and a pint.

ALGERNON. Why is it that at a bachelor's establishment the servants invariably
drink the champagne? I ask merely for information.

LANE. I attribute it to the superior quality of the wine, sir. I have often
observed that in married households the champagne is rarely of a
first-rate brand.

ALGERNON. Good heavens! Is marriage so demoralising as that?

LANE. I believe it IS a very pleasant state, sir. I have had very little
experience of it myself up to the present. I have only been married
once.   That was in consequence of a misunderstanding between
myself and a young person.

ALGERNON. [Languidly.] I don't know that I am much interested in your family
life, Lane.

LANE. No, sir; it is not a very interesting subject. I never think of it myself.

ALGERNON. Very natural, I am sure. That will do, Lane, thank you.

LANE. Thank you, sir. [LANE goes out.]

ALGERNON. Lanes views on marriage seem somewhat lax. Really, if the lower
orders don't set us a good example, what on earth is the use of them?
They seem, as a class, to have absolutely no sense of moral
responsibility.   [Enter LANE.]

LANE. Mr. Ernest Worthing.   [Enter JACK.; LANE goes out.]

ALGERNON. How are you, my dear Ernest? What brings you up to town?

JACK. Oh, pleasure, pleasure! What else should bring one anywhere? Eating as usual, I see, Algy!

ALGERNON. [Stiffly.] I believe it is customary in good society to take some slight refreshment at five o'clock. Where have you been since last Thursday?

JACK. [Sitting down on the sofa.] In the country.

ALGERNON. What on earth do you do there?

JACK. [Pulling off his gloves.] When one is in town one amuses oneself. When one is in the country one amuses other people. It is excessively boring.

ALGERNON. And who are the people you amuse?

JACK. [Airily.] Oh, neighbours, neighbours.

ALGERNON. Got nice neighbours in your part of Shropshire?

JACK. Perfectly horrid! Never speak to one of them.

ALGERNON. How immensely you must amuse them! [Goes over and takes sandwich.] By the way, Shropshire is your county, is it not?

JACK. Eh? Shropshire? Yes, of course. Hallo! Why all these cups? Why cucumber sandwiches? Why such reckless extravagance in one so young? Who is coming to tea?

[O. Wilde]

16. Translating poetry has sometimes been termed as 'the art of the impossible'. Is it really an impossible task? Which are the untranslatable elements in the following lines? Try to suggest possible translations for the second poem.

(a) The Chaos

Dearest creature in creation,
Study English pronunciation.
I will teach you in my verse
Sounds like corpse, corps, horse, and worse.
I will keep you, Suzy, busy,
Make your head with heat grow dizzy.
Tear in eye, your dress will tear.
So shall I! Oh hear my prayer.

Just compare heart, beard, and heard,
Dies and diet, lord and word,
Sword and sward, retain and Britain.

(Mind the latter, how it's written.)
Now I surely will not plague you
With such words as plaque and ague.
But be careful how you speak:
Say break and steak, but bleak and streak;
Cloven, oven, how and low,
Script, receipt, show, poem, and toe.

Billet does not rhyme with ballet,
Bouquet, wallet, mallet, chalet.
Blood and flood are not like food,
Nor is mould like should and would.
Viscous, viscount, load and broad,
Toward, to forward, to reward.
And your pronunciation's OK
When you correctly say croquet,
Rounded, wounded, grieve and sieve,
Friend and fiend, alive and live.

Query does not rhyme with very,
Nor does fury sound like bury.
Dost, lost, post and doth, cloth, loth.
Job, nob, bosom, transom, oath.
Though the differences seem little,
We say actual but victual.
Refer does not rhyme with deafer.
Foeffer does, and zephyr, heifer.
Mint, pint, senate and sedate;
Dull, bull, and George ate late.
Scenic, Arabic, Pacific,
Science, conscience, scientific.

Compare alien with Italian,
Dandelion and battalion.
Sally with ally, yea, ye,
Eye, I, ay, aye, whey, and key.
Say aver, but ever, fever,
Neither, leisure, skein, deceiver.
Heron, granary, canary.
Crevice and device and aerie.

Face, but preface, not efface.
Phlegm, phlegmatic, ass, glass, bass.

Large, but target, gin, give, verging,
Ought, out, joust and scour, scourging.
Ear, but earn and wear and tear
Do not rhyme with here but ere.
Seven is right, but so is even,
Hyphen, roughen, nephew Stephen,
Monkey, donkey, Turk and jerk,
Ask, grasp, wasp, and cork and work.

Pronunciation -- think of Psyche!
Is a paling stout and spikey?
Won't it make you lose your wits,
Writing groats and saying grits?
It's a dark abyss or tunnel:
Strewn with stones, stowed, solace, gunwale,
Islington and Isle of Wight,
Housewife, verdict and indict.

Finally, which rhymes with enough–
Though, through, plough, or dough, or cough?
Hiccough has the sound of cup.
My advice is to give it up!!!

[Gerald Nolst Trenite]

(b)   When I am dead,
        I hope it may be said:
        "his sins were scarlet but his books were red"

[H. Belloc]

17. Translating humorous poetry is also a great challenge for the translator.
    Translate one of the following passages into Spanish, trying to render both
    content and rhyme. Discuss the difficulties presented by the translation and
    explain the way you solved them.

Limericks

There was an Old Man with a flute,
A sarpint ran into his boot;
But he played day and night,
Till the sarpint took flight,
And avoided that man with a flute. [Edward Lear]

These limericks take me so long,
Because rhythm for me is no song;
    but I'll labor and sweat,
    till proficient I get –
I'll just climb there wrong by wrong! [Gunjan Saraf]

While dealing with a poetry section
And working on limerick translation
I can see the awful exam draws near;
And I am feeling all my rising fear;
So I cannot translate with affection. [Ana Fernández]

Eating disorder

Her appetite would take some beating:
She just goes on eating
Ignoring all suggestions
About her digestion:
She binges on cheese,
And Devon cream teas,
Mixing her toasties
With beef, yorkshires, roasties…
And all of that stuff.
It's never enough.
Now, she's round as a ball:
As broad as she's tall;
If she doesn't stop
She'll soon pop.   [Gwyneth Box]

7. Translation and new technologies

7.1. New technologies in translation

Over the last decades we have witnessed a huge growth of information technologies, with the accompanying advantages of speed, effectiveness, ease of use, etc. These new technologies have had a great impact and influence on the translator's task.

Different degrees of human involvement or automation being possible in translation technologies, we can distinguish between the types shown in *Figure 8*, which could be a graphic expression of these different levels of human involvement in the activity of translation.

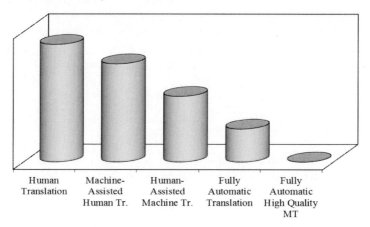

| Human Translation | Machine-Assisted Human Tr. | Human-Assisted Machine Tr. | Fully Automatic Translation | Fully Automatic High Quality MT |

Figure 8: *Degrees of automation in translation technologies.*

Machine or computer-aided translation (MAT/CAT) refers to computer-aided translation with some intervention of a human translator. Depending on the nature of this intervention in the translation, we must differentiate MAHT from HAMT:

- Machine-Assisted Human Translation or Computer Assisted Translation (MAHT/CAT) refers to translation by a human translator with the support of a variety of computerised aids, such as spelling, grammar and style checkers, on-line termbanks, databases, electronic dictionaries, electronic encyclopaedias, etc. The term for all these integrated aids is known as a *translator's workbench*.

- Human-Assisted Machine Translation (HAMT) implies a high degree of automation, with human intervention to disambiguate as necessary, allowing the automatic process to continue; the role of the translator being one or more of the following: (a) pre-editing: to make it possible, or easier, for the program to attempt a translation; (b) interactive editing: to deal with ambiguities as they are encountered, in order to enable the program to proceed; and (c) post-editing: to polish the translation and check for errors.

Fully automatic high quality translation (FAHQT) applies to cases were the SL text is input to the system and the TL text is delivered, both without any involvement of the user. The idea of a translation system that is completely automated and also high quality is still a dream, since it really refers to the ideal machine translation (MT) system that, by just pressing a button, would translate the text as well as (or even better than) a professional translator. Emphasis should be given to the words 'high quality', however, because it all depends on what one understands by *high quality*. If we take it to the absolute, then FAHQT would be a dream not to be realized even in the far future (Fernández Guerra 2000: 22-23).

7.2. Computer-assisted translation

Computer-assisted translation tools are currently the main technology used to meet the needs of the translator. With CAT the computer is like a workstation in which translators have access to a variety of aids, tools and software programs. CAT tools are designed to support and facilitate the translation process, with an enormous saving of time. Even if they do not provide direct translations, they offer a support system that helps translators to find up-to-date information, and to work faster and more accurately. The most important and useful computer tools in the translator's workplace are the following ones:

- Editor software (spell and grammar checkers, which are built into word processing software, but are also available in add-on programs).
- Terminology managers, which allow the translator to create and use a termbank or glossary with the necessary terminology.

- Localization applications, which help to adapt a software, document, or web site product to various markets or localities.
- Electronic dictionaries, glossaries and encyclopaedias, to find definitions and translations of terms and phrases.
- Concordances, to see collocations and contexts in which terms are used.
- On-line bilingual texts, to see previous translations of the same term of phrase.
- Translation Memories, which is another application of on-line bilingual texts.

Electronic dictionaries, mainly those available on-line, as the example in *Figure 9*, are probably the technology that translators use more often. The reason is clear, as it takes less time to type in a word on the computer than to look through a paper dictionary and it is possible to use several dictionaries at the same time. Nowadays there is a huge amount of general dictionaries, specific field or terminology dictionaries, glossaries and databases on the Internet, to name but a few:

- http://www.wordreference.com
- http://www.allwords.com/
- http://www.diccionarios.com/
- http://www.diccionariostraductores.com/
- http://www.thefreedictionary.com/dictionary.htm
- http://www.yourdictionary.com/specialty.html
- Etc.

Concordances can also be particularly valuable. They are word-processing programs that produce a list of all the occurrences of a string of letters within a specific corpus in order to establish patterns that are not always clear, as can be seen in *Figure 10*. Specific functions of these tools include counting word frequencies, making word lists and full concordances, providing statistical data about the number of words or propositions, classifying words, identifying the context in which the words occur, etc. Concordances are quite useful when translating specialized texts with fixed vocabulary and expressions that are normally different between different languages. There are also many online concordancers:

- http://www.antlab.sci.waseda.ac.jp/software.html
- http://www.lexically.net/wordsmith/version5/index.html
- http://www.concordancesoftware.co.uk
- Etc.

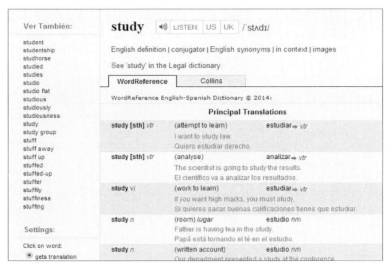

Figure 9: *Example of online dictionary.*

Figure 10: *Example of concordancer.*

On-line bilingual texts are corpora including a SL text and its translation, previously carried out by human translators. They are also called bilingual corpus or bi-text and can be useful to facilitate later translations, since they supply ready solutions to fixed expressions and formulaic language, like in the example reproduced in *Figure 11*.

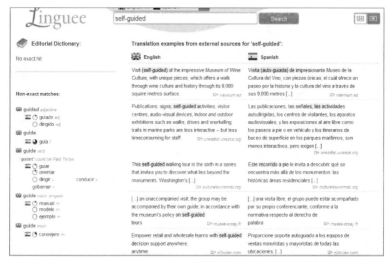

Figure 11: *Example of online bilingual corpus.*

Translation memories are one of the most important applications of online bilingual texts. In this case the memory is made with the translator's self work, and the translator stores in a database translations for future re-use. Translation memory programs record bilingual pairs consisting of a SL segment combined with a TL segment. Whenever an identical or similar SL segment appears again, the program will automatically suggest the previous translation. This tool can be extremely useful and save the translator valuable time when translating texts that are quite similar, with terminological and phraseological homogeneity. Software such as *Trados* or *Translator manager* are easy to use, but we can also find examples of online publicly accessible translation memories (see the example of *Figure 12*):

- http://glosbe.com/tmem/
- http://aligner.abbyyonline.com/en
- http://mymemory.translated.net/
- http://ipsc.jrc.ec.europa.eu/index.php?id=197
- Etc.

Figure 12: *Example of translation memories.*

7.3. Machine translation

"Machine translation is the application of computers to the translation of texts from one natural language into another" (Hutchins, 1986: 15). MT involves the substitution of the role of humans in the actual translation process by the use of computer software; and is now used to define computerised systems that carry out language translation, whether they are fully automated or require further human assistance. MT aims at replacing, to some extent, the need for human translation (for some kind of texts); but a human translator is always needed to edit what is translated by MT systems. Currently, MT is mainly a valuable tool to aid in human translation.

7.3.1. The need for MT

The need for MT is clear. Nowadays, there seems to be a great demand for translation and investment on MT systems to obtain faster and cheaper translations. The competitive world markets have a need for high quality translation of their products, research, etc.; and supranational organisations have indeed mountains of paperwork to translate. Besides, in organisations like the European Union (EU) and the United Nations (UN); or in countries like Canada, Switzerland, Belgium, etc.; or in communities within the same country

(Wales, Catalonia, etc.), multilingualism is a fact of everyday life, and there is a limit on how far human translators productivity can be increased without automation. Needless to say, MT is extremely important in such contexts.

- *Commercial importance*: translation is necessary and it is expensive. It is a highly skilled job, translators' salaries are quite high, and delays are normal. Let us just mention that a human translator can translate an average of 20 pages per day, whilst some of the modern MT systems can produce about 20 million translated pages in the same period of time. With such a tremendous difference in mind, human translators could very well be compared to medieval scribes, while MT could perhaps be compared to the most modern printing press (Fernández Guerra 2000: 24).
- *Scientifically*, MT is important also because it means development in computer science, applied linguistics and artificial intelligence.
- *Philosophically* it is very challenging as well, since the extent to which one can automate translation is an indication of the extent to which one can automate thinking (Arnold et al, 1994: 5).

For the time being, however, the real use of MT is not much. Despite the advances of MT, these translations only represent about 2% of the total translations carried out over the world. The aim of MT is to achieve faster and cheaper translations, but what current automatic translation programmes offer is the following:

- Acceptable (or even high quality) translation of input texts written in a naturally occurring sublanguage or in an artificial controlled language.
- The possibility of getting raw translations of texts that belong to certain fields of knowledge and that, after a revision, can produce high quality translations;
- Raw translations that can be understood by specialists in that field of knowledge, without needing any changes (because it is not going to be published, for instance).

Unfortunately, there are many limitations within MT. Problems are due to the fact that MT systems are still unable to deal adequately with context, ambiguity, semantics, polysemy, homography, anaphora, idioms, and the like, because not all the necessary linguistic information can be installed in the software, and because the program needs some human interaction during the translation process to deal with problems, to mention just some of the shortcomings. Fernández Guerra (2000: 98) mentions some striking MT howlers:

- The Parker Company, for example, promised that no one carrying one of their pens in their pocket would be embarrassed; in Mexico, the company promised "no embarazar a quien los llevara en el bolsillo".
- The Spanish *EFE* press agency, in Catalonia, once translated a subtitle "La fiscal endurece las penas" as "La fiscal endureix penes".
- The paper Segre, in Lleida, came out in Catalan once translating "Un herido en la unidad de curas intesivas" as "capellans intensius".
- *El periódico de Cataluña: Lady Di* as "Leidi Vaig Donar", or *Isabel Tocino* as "Isabel Cansalada".

7.3.2. How MT works

The machine translation internals are the applications that perform the translation. MT internals (or MT systems) can be classified according to the overall processing organisation or the abstract arrangement of their processing modules (or their strategy). Considering the complexity of that overall processing organization, as well as the various approaches to MT research, we can distinguish the types outlined in *Figure 13*.

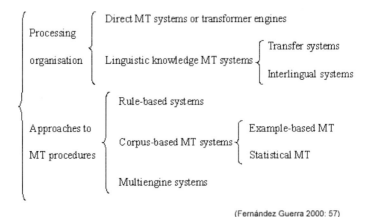

(Fernández Guerra 2000: 57)

Figure 13: *Types of MT.*

Direct MT systems or transformer engines are the most rudimentary ones in their technology (dating from the first experiments in the 1960s). These systems include a bilingual dictionary of lexical correspondences and phrases or expressions; and some basic rules to re-order words (that roughly re-arrange their order to suit the rules of the target language).

Transfer systems were developed in the 1980s, with more sophisticated MT engines. These systems work using 3 main automatic components:

- The analyser or *parser* analyses the sentence with the SL grammars available and produces their abstract representation (lexical, syntactic and semantic).
- Once the analysis tree has been done, the system applies syntactic *transfer* rules that turn the grammatical information of a language into the most appropriate structure in the TL.
- Finally, the *generator* of structures translates the sentence (with TL grammars) from the TL interface structure into the final TL text output.

Interlingual systems translate texts using a deeper level of representation, called interlingua, which is supposed to be an abstract representation of both the SL and the TL texts; that is, this interlingual representation should be neutral to any language and thus break the direct relationship that a bilingual dictionary approach would have (they are actually representations of *meaning*, in a most abstract sense). However, to create a language independent representation of word meaning seems to pose many problems as regards the representation of meaning and concepts. Besides, to use an interlingua in MT can lead to unnecessary work, since it can be easier (and maybe more reliable) to use a transfer system: for example, in the case of texts with simple structure, such an abstract representation can be extra and unnecessary work.

Rule-based approaches are translation systems based on linguistic information about source and target languages basically retrieved from bilingual dictionaries and grammars covering the main semantic, morphological, and syntactic regularities of each language. The rule-based approach includes transfer-based MT, interlingual MT and dictionary-based MT systems.

In corpus-based approaches statistical machine translation tries to generate translations using statistical methods based on bilingual text corpora. They take as data very large corpora of machine readable translated text that can be used to train a statistics-based MT system.

Finally, hybrid MT approaches are multiengine systems that leverage the strengths of statistical and rule-based translation methodologies. Research is being carried out at different centres to (automatically or semi-automatically) annotate corpus resources with various types of linguistic information, in addition to grammatical tagging, prosodic annotation (indicating features of stress and annotation), syntactic tagging (indicating phrasal groups of words); semantic and discourse level tagging (indicating anaphoric and other similar links).

7.3.3. Free on-line MT systems

We should also mention, due to its widespread use and how the Internet has proven to be a huge stimulus for MT, free on-line MT systems. The first free online MT system was AltaVista's Babel Fish (launched in 1997), but there are now many others, and they include many pairs of languages:

- https://translate.google.com/
- http://www.reverso.net/text_translation.aspx?lang=ES
- http://www.systranet.com/translate
- http://translation2.paralink.com/
- http://www.worldlingo.com/
- http://www.freetranslation.com/
- http://translate.reference.com/
- http://www.alphaworks.ibm.com
- http://www.elingo.com
- http://translation.babylon.com/
- Etc.

However, we should be cautious, since translations obtained with these systems are rather poor, since they use simple grammars and parsers, limited dictionaries, and are only useful to know the meaning of some words and for very simple structures with a restricted vocabulary and, undoubtedly, not recommended as a translation tool. Suffice to see the examples in *Figure 14*.

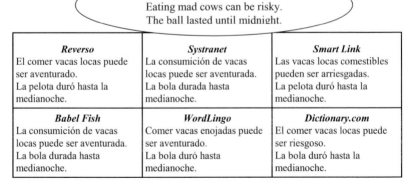

Reverso	*Systranet*	*Smart Link*
El comer vacas locas puede ser aventurado. La pelota duró hasta la medianoche.	La consumición de vacas locas puede ser aventurada. La bola durada hasta medianoche.	Las vacas locas comestibles pueden ser arriesgadas. La pelota duró hasta la medianoche.
Babel Fish	*WordLingo*	*Dictionary.com*
La consumición de vacas locas puede ser aventurada. La bola durada hasta medianoche.	Comer vacas enojadas puede ser aventurado. La bola duró hasta medianoche.	El comer vacas locas puede ser riesgoso. La bola duró hasta la medianoche.

Figure 14: *Results obtained with free on-line MT systems.*

7.4. Further readings

Craciunescu, O., C. Gerding-Salas, and S. Stringer-O'Keeffe. 2004. Machine Translation and Computer-Assisted Translation: a New Way of Translating? *Translation Journal,* Volume 8, No. 3.

Garspari, F. And J. Hutchins. 2007. Online and free! Ten years of online machine translation: origins, developments, current use and future prospects. *MT Summit XI, Copenhagen, Denmark, 10-14 September 2007, Proceedings*: 199-206.

Hutchins, J. 2001. Machine translation and human translation: in competition or in complementation? *International Journal of Translation* 13: 5-20.

Ulitkin, I. 2011. Computer-assisted Translation Tools: A brief review. *Translation Journal,* Volume 15, No. 1.

7.5. Tasks

1. Have a look at the following sentences. How could they be translated? Which problems could an MT program encounter?

    (1) Turn on the light.

    (2) Light my fire, please.

    (3) A light blue shirt.

    (4) Eating mad cows can be risky.

    (5) To eat mad cows can be unhealthy.

    (6) Mad cows that are eating can be fearful (since they can react in an unpredictable manner).

    (7) It's a lie that you lie.

    (8) I cook, so I'm a cook.

    (9) The hands of a clock.

    (10) The apple of the eye.

    (11) Jane kicked the bucket.

    (12) I'm a heavy smoker, and you're a heavy student.

    (13) The ball rolled down the hill.

    (14) The ball lasted until midnight.

2. Now try any on-line MT program and analyse its translations. The following are some free on-line translators:

- Reverso: http://www.reverso.net/text_translation.aspx?lang=ES
- Systran: http://www.systranet.com/translate
- Smart Link Corporation: http://translation2.paralink.com/
- AltaVista Babel Fish - Babel Fish Translation: http://es.babelfish.yahoo.com/
- Worldlingo - Free Online Translations: http://www.worldlingo.com/
- SDL International: http://www.freetranslation.com/
- Dictionary.com - Machine Translation: http://translate.reference.com/

3. Analyse the following translations. Both programs "Power Translator Pro" and "Systran Multitranslate Utility" were said to be high quality MT programs. Do you agree? Which percentage of (in)appropriate translations have these programs produced?

ST	Power Translator Pro	Systran Multitranslate
TAPAS Y BEBIDAS	TAPAS AND DRINKS	COVERS AND DRINKS
Pulpo a la feria	Octopus to the fair	Squid to the fair
Patatas bravas	Brave potatoes	Brave potatoes
Calamares	Squids	Calamaries
Cañas y chiquitos.	Canes and tiny	Very small canes and
Gazpacho casero.	Homemade gazpacho.	Homemade Gazpacho.
Agua de valencia.	Valency water.	Water of valence.
Jamón pata negra.	Ham black paw.	Jamón black leg.
Fabada asturiana.	Asturian Fabada.	Asturian Fabada.

Beba en bota y en porrón	Drink in boot and in jug	Drink in boot and porrón
Fino Tío Pepe	I die Uncle Pepe	Fine Uncle Pepe
Fino Quinta	Fine Fifth	Fine Quinta
Pacharán de Navarra	Pacharán of Navarrese	Pacharán of Navarre
Vino de Rioja y Valdepeñas	Wine of Rioja and Valdepeñas	Wine of Rioja and Valdepeñas
MENÚ DE HOY	MENU OF TODAY	TODAY MENU
Judías con chorizo	Jews with sausage	Bean with garlic sausage
Bonito a la plancha	Beautiful to the iron	Pretty to the plate
PROMOCIÓN DE APERTURA	PROMOTION OF OPENING	OPENING PROMOTION
Una jarra de sangría al pedir un Pepito de ternera	A jar of sangria when requesting a veal Pepito	A jar of drain when requesting a Pepito of calf
ACTIVIDADES PARA ANIMAR LA VELADA	ACTIVITIES TO ENCOURAGE THE VEILED ONE	ACTIVITIES TO ANIMATE THE EVENING
Concurso de futbolín	Futbolín competition	Aid of futbolín
Torneo de dominó	I lathe of domino	Match of dominated
Porra de lotería primitiva	Club of primitive lottery	Club of primitive lottery
Concurso de tute por parejas	Tute competition for even	Aid of tute by pairs
Barajas disponibles para jugar en las mesas	You shuffle available to play in the tables	Barajas available to play in the tables
Toca el piano cada tarde.	He/she plays the piano every afternoon.	It touches the piano late each.
Lady Di quiere otro niño.	Lady gave another boy he/she wants.	Lady Di loves another boy.
Entre y tome asiento.	Among and have a seat.	Between and it takes seat.
This diet has been established according to your daily eating habits.	Esta dieta se ha establecido según sus hábitos comiendo diarios.	Esta dieta se ha establecido según sus hábitos diarios el comer.
We must polish the Polish furniture.	Nosotros debemos pulir el mobiliario polaco.	Polacos de los muebles de los los del pulir de Debemos.
The soldier decided to desert his dessert in the desert.	El soldado decidió abandonar su postre en el desierto.	Desierto abandonar del EL del postre del su del decidía del soldado del EL.
They were too close to the door to close it.	Ellos también estaban cerca de la puerta al cierre él.	Estaban también el cerrarla de cerca de la puerta párrafo.
Use the same procedure all the time, because water in the fuel system can freeze during winter or summer. Loosen the pivot fasteners of the dynamo or alternator	Use el mismo procedimiento todo el tiempo, porque el agua en el sistema de combustible puede helar durante invierno o verano. Suelte los broches del pivote	Utilizar el mismo procedimiento toda la hora, porque el agua en el sistema de carburante puede congelar durante invierno o verano. Aflojar los sujetadores del

mounting. Loosen also the fasteners of the adjustment link.	del dínamo o montura del alternador. También suelte los broches del eslabón de ajuste.	pivote del montaje del dínamo o del alternador. Aflojar también los sujetadores del acoplamiento del ajuste.
Normally the text does include instructions to clean joint faces or to renew joints. These operations must be done, if necessary.	Normalmente el texto incluye las instrucciones para limpiar las caras de la juntura o renovar las junturas. Estos funcionamientos deben hacerse, si necesario.	El texto incluye normalmente instrucciones de limpiar caras comunes o de renovar empalmes. Estas operaciones se deben hacer, en caso de necesidad.
Special courts may be established by law for the trial of offences in cases where it may be determined in accordance with such law that the ordinary courts are inadequate to secure the effective the effective administration of justice, and the preservation of public peace and order. The constitution, powers, jurisdiction and procedure of such special courts shall be prescribed by law.	· que las cortes Especiales pueden ser establecidas por la ley para el ensayo de ofensas en casos dónde puede determinarse de acuerdo con la tal ley que las cortes ordinarias son inadecuadas afianzar el eficaz la administración eficaz de justicia, y la preservación de paz pública y orden. La constitución, poderes, jurisdicción y procedimiento de tales cortes especiales serán prescritas por la ley.	Las cortes especiales se pueden establecer por la ley para el ensayo de ofensas en los casos donde puede ser determinado de acuerdo con tal ley que las cortes ordinarias son inadecuadas asegurar el eficaz la administración eficaz de la justicia, y la preservación de la paz y de la orden públicas. La constitución, las energías, la jurisdicción y el procedimiento de tales cortes especiales serán prescritos por la ley.

4.   Revise the articles in section 7.4., dealing with the theoretical contents of this chapter. Which are the main capabilities and limitations of current automatic translation programs and computer-aided translation tools?

8. The evaluation of translation

8.1. Difficulty in the evaluation of translations

A good number of studies deal with translation evaluation, translation quality assessment, translation criticism, judgment, etc. Translation evaluation is without doubt very important, but also a complicated and risky process. Translators themselves evaluate when they chose the options they think are best for their TL text. Evaluating someone else's translation is also necessary: trainee translators, professionals, clients, translatologists, etc. all agree about the need for a translation to be *good* and *adequate*. Establishing what is *good* or *bad*, however, is quite complex, and there are no globally accepted objective criteria to assess translations, though there are many well-known proposals, like the SICAL (by the Federal Bureau of Translation), the scale BEST (Binghamton Evaluation Scale for Translation), the scale SEVTE (Spanish into English Verbatim Translation Exam), and many other studies that tackle the evaluation of translation (Newmark 1991, Hatim and Mason 1997, House 2005, Nord 1991, etc.). There are also several counterarguments and criticism against the proposals published (see Fernández Guerra 2002). Some theoreticians even escape the problem of how to assess and evaluate translations, arguing that true objective evaluations are not possible. The personality of the translator, his likes and dislikes, or his linguistic preferences, for example, may not coincide at all with the personality of the *critic* or the one who is supposed to evaluate or assess the translation.

So as not to bite off more than we can chew, I propose to focus our attention on the difficulties mentioned by Williams (2009: 5-7), who focused on the following problems when evaluating translations or designing any translation quality assessment model:

- Evaluator (whether the one evaluating the TL text has the linguistic or subject-field knowledge required).
- Level of target language rigour (some evaluators consider elegant style essential, for instance, but not others).
- Seriousness of errors of transfer (some evaluators will ignore minor variations, while others will prefer total fidelity to the SL text).

- Sampling versus full-text analysis (fully analysing only a sample of the translations instead of the whole text).

- Quantification of quality (micro-textual analysis of samples to provide error counts).

- Levels of seriousness of error (differences between evaluators when grading errors by seriousness levels).

- Multiple levels of assessment (different parameters to assess the quality of a translation, such as accuracy, TL quality, register, situational features, etc.).

- Translation quality assessment purpose or function (what to assess will also differ depending on the aim of the translation and the aim of the evaluation).

After mentioning problems when evaluating translations, Mobaraki and Aminzadeh (2012: 64) maintain that four factors should be necessary: *validity* (suitability of the method to the defined situation of evaluation to be verified), *reliability* (usability of the method to the similar situations to be confirmed), *objectivity* (the validity and reliability of the method for the intended situation to be exemplified and proved), and *systematicity* (defining a clear framework for evaluation).

8.2. Main approaches to the evaluation of translations

There are many types of evaluation of translations: quantitative (based on statistical measurement, normally of errors made), qualitative (based on readers' response), holistic (an overall impression instead of relying on a points-based scale), diagnostic (to determine areas for improvement), formative (normally to measure students' progress and provide feedback), summative (to measure the results of learning), etc. And traditional proposals to the evaluation of translations focused on three main aspects:

1. Evaluation of the TL text as any other original text written in the TL. This is the case of "consumer translations", that are aimed at the general public (no matter what the text is about), in which fluency is more important than fidelity.

2. Evaluation of the TL text as compared with the SL text. This implies taking specific passages or pieces of the text and indicating errors in "content" or in "syntax", which was mainly a linguistic evaluation. For evaluations of this

kind the translator should try to reproduce, as close as possible, all that appears in the SL text, at all levels of analysis.

3. Evaluation of TL text as part of the historical evolution of the TL, within literary criticism. This usually implies the case in which the translation was made time ago (in another period of evolution of the TL, and the need for a new one was underlined, like in the case of Luther's *Bible*, for example (Fernández Guerra 2002).

The risk in most evaluations is that the critic tends to concentrate on the *howlers*, not valuing the achievements at all. And, of course, the validity (even avoiding to concentrate on howlers) depends on the number of specific linguistic, extra-linguistic, cultural, etc. elements compared. Certain "scientific" method or certain "rules" are definitely needed, so as to assess translations correctly. But usually theoreticians only give us very general guidelines, like comprehension of the TL text by an average reader, establishing areas and levels of analysis (morpheme, sentence, structural units, ...), analysing the appropriateness of translation procedures, analysing the translator's linguistic competence, recurring to back translations, etc. House (2001, 2005) summarizes fairly well the main four main approaches to translation quality assessment:

- Intuitive and subjective approaches: models following this approach tend to see the quality of the TL text as dependent on the translator's knowledge, intuitions and competences, consisting of assessments like "there is something lost in the translation" and normally based on global opinions and appraisals made by the evaluator or critic.

- Response oriented, psycholinguistic approaches: these approaches focus on dynamic equivalence between the SL and the TL text, and appraise whether TL readers will react in the same way as SL readers did. She mentions intelligibility and informativeness as main issues followed by proponents of this approach. However, it is certainly difficult to evaluate and measure what could be considered as an equivalent response by someone in particular or by a group of people. Besides, when evaluating a translation of a SL text, it seems wise to compare it to the SL text, which is largely ignored in these methods.

- Text and discourse based approaches: these normally follow linguistic, comparative literature and functional models. Linguistic approaches compare pairs of SL and TL items, in order to analyse syntactic, semantic, structural, stylistic, orthographic and pragmatic regularities of transfer. Models focusing on comparative literature focus on the function of the translation in the system of the TL literature, culture and power relations, only dealing with the SL remotely, since it is of minor significance. And functional models focus on the *skopos* or aim of the translation, assessing whether the TL text fulfils the same aim or communicative function of the SL text. Again, determining equivalence and adequacy in the translation is not easy, since it all depends on the aim of the translation, the audience, etc.

- Functional-pragmatic approaches: House's proposal (that can be seen in several well-known publications, shortened in House 2001, 2005) focuses on pragmatic theories of language use, analysing linguistic and situational particularities of both SL and TL texts, like different levels of language, register or genre. She mentions dimensional mismatches as pragmatic errors dealing with the use of language in specific speech communities, and non-dimensional mismatches that involve denotative differences at various levels. Her proposal is displayed in *Figure 15* (House 2001: 249).

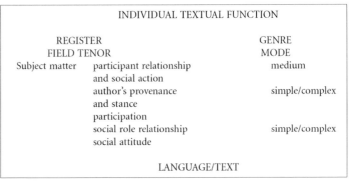

Figure 15: *House's analytic model.*

8.3. Criteria for assessment

Evaluators usually focus on either a micro-analytical or a macro-analytical level, and will give more importance to some issues, like lexical, stylistic or structural equivalence, ideology, text function, register, appropriate translation techniques, etc. Evaluators will always have their own preferences, since value judgements can occur whenever we read a SL text or a TL text. Trying to be coherent and determine a good and comprehensive way to evaluate translations is essential. It all depends on the aim of the translation and the translation audience. When dealing with translations carried out by students, for instance, many factors need to be taken into account, like considering whether they recognize translation problems, how these are solved, or their language level, for example.

Some scholars and translation lecturers just focus on translation errors, and how to penalise those errors, which is widely criticised but, as Kussmaul (1995) suggests, it can be useful to classify types of errors and translation difficulties. Of course, clear criteria should be established when analysing the possible translation errors.

Nord (2001: 73-8) considers that translation errors are inadequate solutions to a translation problem, and classifies these errors into four types: (1) pragmatic translation errors, such as lack of receiver orientation, (2) cultural translation errors, due to an inadequate decision with regard to reproduction or adaption of culture-specific conventions, (3) linguistic translation errors, caused by an inadequate translation when the focus is on language structures, and (4) text-specific translation errors, related to a text-specific translation problem which can be evaluated from a functional or pragmatic point of view.

Following those 4 aspects that can lead to translation problems, as well as some proposals for the evaluation of translations (Fernández Guerra 2002), a taxonomy including ten aspects to be taken into account when analysing students' errors and achievements has been established, focusing both on isolated units and on a macro-analysis of the translation. Of course, when evaluating these issues, one needs to take into account three things: (1) that errors can be more or less significant, (2) that creative solutions to translation problems, offering good and adequate translations, should also be considered, and (3) that some factors can make the evaluation vary, like the receiver, the purpose of the translation, the use of tools such as dictionaries, the time available to carry out the translation, etc.

- Lexico-semantic aspects (LEX): different meaning or use of inappropriate equivalents in the TL that do not capture exactly the same meaning of the SL term, or wrong translation of specialized terminology, formulaic language, initials or abbreviations.

- Morpho-syntactic aspects (GR): grammar mistakes, inappropriate word order or sentence structure.

- Spelling and punctuation aspects (TIP): including typographical differences between the SL and the TL, like the use of 'em dashes' in Spanish for dialogues and quotation marks in English.

- Cultural-bound words (CULT): not being aware of differences between both cultures, or not using the most suitable strategies for dealing with a cultural gap.

- Pragmatic aspects (PRAG): inadequacies can arise from the differences in extralinguistic situations, socio-linguistic norms or language usage, which can deal with factors such as sender, receiver, medium, time, place, text function, inadequacy to the translation aim, etc.

- Writing style and register (STY); this includes trying to reproduce the same degree of formality, or considerations such as variations of register, adequacy of the social, geographical or temporal dialects or sociolects, and stylistic devices, such as rhyme, alliterations, puns, emphasis, etc.

- Textual cohesion and coherence (TEXT), or logical flow of information and naturalness in the TL text.

- Changes in content (CONT), including either addition or omission of SL terms or content.

- Translation technique (TECH): Coherence and appropriateness in the way translation techniques (or transfer strategies and re-wording) are used all over the text.

- Overall assessment at a communicative level (AS).

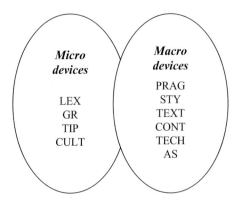

Figure 16: *Aspects to be evaluated.*

8.4. Further readings

Fernández Guerra, A. 2002. Evaluación de la traducción: la herencia del siglo XX. *SELL: Studies in English Language and Linguistics*, 4: 89-144.

House, J. 2001. Translation Quality Assessment: Linguistic Description versus Social Evaluation. *Meta: Translators' Journal*, 46: 243-257.

House, J. 2005. Quality of Translation. In Baker, M. (ed.) *Routledge Encyclopedia of Translation Studies*. London and New York: Routledge.

Mohsen Mobaraki, M. and S. Aminzadeh. 2012. A Study on Different Translation Evaluation Strategies to Introduce an Eclectic Method. *International Journal of English Linguistics*, 2: 63-70.

Williams, M. 2009. Translation Quality Assessment. *Mutatis Mutandis*, 2: 3-23.

8.5. Tasks

1. Read through the following passage from *Hamlet* and the translations reproduced.

   (a) Compare linguistic and situational peculiarities of source and target texts.

   (b) Analyse target texts' stylistic naturalness and functional equivalence.

   (c) Recur to 'back translations' (i.e. translate one of the target texts back into English) and try to find reasons for resulting deviations from the source text.

ST: *Hamlet*

HAMLET: No, good mother. Here's metal more attractive.

POLONIUS: O ho! Do you mark that?

HAMLET: Lady, shall I lie in your lap?

OPHELIA: No, my lord.

HAMLET: I mean, my head upon your lap.

OPHELIA: Ay, my lord.

HAMLET: Do you think I mean country matters?

OPHELIA: I think nothing, my lord.

HAMLET: That's a fair thought to lie between maids' legs.

OPHELIA: What is, my lord?

HAMLET: Nothing.

OPHELIA: You are merry, my lord?

[Shakespeare]

TT 1: *Molina Foix*	**TT 2:** *Conejero*
H: No, madre mía, hay aquí un imán que me tira más.	H: No, querida madre. Que hay por ahí imán más atractivo.
P: ¿Reparásteis en eso?	P: Hola! ¡Hola! ¿Habéis oído eso?
H: ¿Señora, puedo echarme en tus rodillas?	H: ¿Me dejáis poner la cabeza en vuestro regazo?
O: No, mi señor.	O: No, mi señor
H: Quiero decir reposando la cabeza sobre tus rodillas.	H: Tan sólo he dicho la cabeza... en el regazo.
O: Sí, mi señor.	O: Sí, mi señor.
H: Pensaste que mis ideas eran tan bajas.	H: ¿Qué otra cosa pensasteis que tenía en la cabeza?
O: No pienso en cosa alguna, mi señor.	O: No pensé nada, mi señor.
H: Buen pensamiento para posarse entre las piernas de una doncella.	H: Bello pensamiento entre las piernas de una doncella.
O: ¿Cuál, mi señor?	O: ¿Cómo, mi señor?
H: La cosa alguna.	H: Nada.
O: Qué ganas de diversión, señor.	O: Estáis de buen humor, mi señor.

2. Analyse the poem beneath and its translations. Pay particular attention to the diachronic features of the language, all the meanings and associations of meanings, and the poem's metre and rhyme.

   (a) Did the translators focus on some elements at the expense of others?

   (b) Do the translations reflect an individual reading, interpretation and selection of criteria?

ST: *Air and Angels*

Twice or thrice had I loved thee,
Before I knew thy face or name,
So in a voice, so in a shapelesse flame.
Angells affect us oft, and worship'd bee;

Still when, to where thou wert, I came,
Some lovely glorious nothing I did see.
But since my soule, whose child love is,
Takes limmes of flesh, and else could nothing doe,
More sutile the parent is,

Love must not be, but take a body too,

And therefore what thy wert, and who,
I bid Love aske, and now
That it assume thy body, I allow,
And fixe it selfe in thy lip, eye, and brow.

              [J. Donne]

TT 1: J. B. Álvarez-Buylla

Dos o tres veces, antes te habré amado,
De haber tu nombre y cara conocido;
Tal un Angel en llamas trascendido
Nos afecta y reclama ser loado,
Pero cuando a tu lado yo he venido,
Sólo un nada adorable he contemplado.
Mas si mi alma, y su hijo amor,
En carne se substancia, o si no es nada,
Debe amor imitar a su hacedor
Y convertirse en forma substanciada.
Por eso yo a mi amor le preguntaba
Por ti, y ya le he permitido
Que su ser en tu cuerpo sea asumido
Y se fije en tu rostro convertido.

TT 2: Puri Ribes

Dos o tres veces a ti te hube amado,
antes de que tu rostro o nombre conociera.
Así, en una voz, en una llama informe,
a menudo los *ángeles* nos mueven y son reverenciados.
Cuando, hacia donde estabas yo acudía,
una gloriosa, encantadora, nada, percibía.
Pero, puesto que mi alma, cuyo hijo es el amor,
sus miembros toma de la carne, y nada de otro modo hacer podría,
más sutil que su padre
no debe el amor ser, sino tomar también un cuerpo.
Y así, lo que tú fuiste, y quién,
pedí al Amor que preguntara, y ahora
que tu cuerpo asuma, yo autorizo,
y que en tu labio se fije, y en tu ojo, y en tu ceja.

3. Your role will now be that of a writer, translator and assessor or critic.

(a) You first have to *write* (create yourself) a short text (five or eight lines will be enough) that includes several difficulties or *untranslatable* elements, such as idioms, rhyme, palindromes, colloquialisms, culture-specific terms, etc.

(b) Pair up and exchange texts. You now have to *translate* your partner's creation.

(c) Once you get your partner's translation of your text, you have to *assess* it. Use the evaluation scale in your dossier. Analyse your partner's receptivity in the SL and his/her capacity to reproduce it in the TL. Do not only concentrate on the howlers, you also need to value the achievements. Remember that, in the case of wrong or inappropriate translations, you must provide alternative options.

References

Alcaraz Varó, E. and M.A. Martínez Linares. 1997. *Diccionario de lingüística moderna*. Barcelona: Ariel.

Arnold, D. et al. 1994. *Machine Translation. An Introductory Guide*. Oxford: NCC Blackwell Ltd.

Baker, M. 1992. *In other words. A coursebook on translation*. London: Routledge.

Baker, M. and G. Saldanha (eds.). 2011. *Routledge Encyclopedia of Translation Studies*. London: Routledge.

Barbe, K. 1996. The dichotomy free and literal translation. *Meta*, 41: 328-337.

Bassnett, S. 2014. *Translation Studies*. New York: Routledge.

Bassnett-McGuire, S. 1988. *Translation Studies*. London: Routledge.

Bassnett-McGuire, S. 1998. The translation turn in cultural studies. In Bassnett McGuire and Lefevere (eds.) *Constructing Cultures: Essays on Literary Translation*. Clevedon: Multilingual Matters, 123-140.

Belloc, H. 1931. *On Translation*. Oxford: Clarendon.

Bernardini, S. 2001. Think-aloud protocols in translation research: Achievements, limits, future prospects. *Target,* 13: 241–263.

Bly, R. 1982. The Eight Stages of Translation. *The Kenyon Review*, Vol. 4, No. 2: 68-89.

Borges, J.L. 1957. Versiones Homéricas. *Discusión*. Buenos Aires: Emecé: 108-109.

Brower, R.A. (ed.). 1966 (1959). *On Translation*. Cambridge: Harvard University Press.

Bühler, K. 1934. *Sprachtheorie: Die Darstellungsfunition der Sprache.* Sttutgart: Fischer.

Campbell, S. 1999. A Cognitive Approach to Source Text Difficulty in Translation. *Target* 11: 33-63.

Catford, J.C. 1965. *A Linguistic Theory of Translation.* Oxford: University Press.

Cerdá Massó, R. 1986. *Diccionario de lingüística*. Madrid: Anaya.

Chesterman, A. 1997. *Memes of translation: the spread of ideas in translation theory*. Amsterdam and Philadelphia: John Benjamins.

Collins. 2000. *Collins English Dictionary*. London: Collins.

Craciunescu, O., C. Gerding-Salas and S. Stringer-O'Keeffe. 2004. Machine Translation and Computer-Assisted Translation: a New Way of Translating? *Translation Journal,* Volume 8, No. 3.

de Pedro, R. 1999. The translatability of texts: A historical overview. *Meta*, 44: 547-559.

Dechao, L. 2011. Think-aloud teaching in translation class: implications from TAPs translation research. *Perspectives: Studies in Translatology*, 19: 109-122.

Delisle, J. 1988. *Translation: An Interpretative Approach.* Ottawa & London: University of Ottawa Press.

Dollerup, C. 2006. *Basics of Translation Studies*. Iasi: Institutul European.

Fernández Guerra, A. 2000. *Machine Translation: Capabilities and Limitations*. Valencia: Publicaciones de la Universitat de València.

Fernández Guerra, A. 2001. *El arte de traducir y la máquina de traducir. Antagonismo o síntesis integradora*. Valencia: Albatros.

Fernández Guerra, A. 2002. Evaluación de la traducción: la herencia del siglo XX. *SELL: Studies in English Language and Linguistics*, 4: 89-144.

Fernández Guerra, A. 2003. La traducción a debate: cuestiones polémicas. In *Homenaje al Dr. D. José M Ruiz Ruiz*. Valladolid: Publicaciones de la Universidad de Valladolid, 119-164.

Fernández Guerra, A. 2004. *Traducción inglés-español en la licenciatura en Filología Inglesa. Proyecto docente e investigador*. Castellón: Universitat Jaume I.

Fernández Guerra, A. 2012a. The issue of (un)translatability revisited: theoretical and practical perspectives. *Forum. International Journal of Translation Studies*, 10.2: 35-60.

Fernández Guerra, A. 2012b. Crossing Boundaries: The Translation of Cultural Referents in English and Spanish. *Word and Text. A Journal of Literary Studies and Linguistics*, Vol. II: 121-138.

Fernández Guerra, A. 2014. The usefulness of translation in foreign language learning: students' attitudes. *International Journal of English Language & Translation Studies*: 153-170.

Fernández, F. 1993. *Historia de la lengua inglesa*. Madrid: Gredos.

García Yebra, V. 1970. *Prólogo* a su edición de Aristóteles *Metafísica* (ed. Trilingüe). Madrid: Gredos.

García Yebra, V. 1982. *Teoría y práctica de la Traducción*. Madrid: Gredos.

Garspari, F. and J. Hutchins. 2007. Online and free! Ten years of online machine translation: origins, developments, current use and future prospects. *MT Summit XI, Copenhagen, Denmark, 10-14 September 2007, Proceedings*: 199-206.

Gentzler, E. 1993. *Contemporary Translation Theories*. London: Routledge.

Graedler, A.L. 2000. Cultural shock. In Oslo *Studies in English on the Net - Translation course*. Oslo: University of Oslo.

Hale, S. and S. Campbell. 2002. The interaction between text difficulty and translation accuracy. *Babel*, 48: 14-33.

Halverson, S. 2009. Psycholinguistic and cognitive approaches. In Baker, M. and G. Saldana (eds.): 211-217.

Hartmann, R.K.K. and F.C. Stork. 1976. *Dictionary of Language and Linguistics*. London: Applied Science Publishers.

Harvey, M. 2012. A beginner's course in legal translation: the case of culture-bound terms. Tradulex.org. *Genève 2000: Actes. La traduction juridique. Histoire, théorie(s) et pratique*.

Hatim, B and J. Munday. 2004. *Translation: An advanced resource book*. New York: Routledge.

Hatim, B. and I. Mason. 1990. *Discourse and the translator*. London: Longman.

Hatim, B. and I. Mason. 1997. *The Translator as Communicator*. London: Routledge.

Holmes, J.S. 1972. The Name and Nature of Translation Studies; expanded version in *Translated! Papers on Literary Translation and Translation Studies*. Amsterdam: Rodopi (1988): 66-80.

House, J. 2001. Translation Quality Assessment: Linguistic Description versus Social Evaluation. *Meta: Translators' Journal*, 46: 243-257.

House, J. 2005. Quality of Translation. In Baker, M. (ed.) *Routledge Encyclopedia of Translation Studies*. London and New York: Routledge.

Hurtado Albir, A. (dir.). 1999. *Enseñar a traducir. Metodología en la formación de traductores e intérpretes. Teoría y fichas prácticas.* Madrid: Edelsa.

Hurtado Albir, A. (ed.). 1994. *Estudis sobre la traducció.* Castellón: Publicacions de la Universitat Jaume I.

Hurtado Albir, A. 2001. *Traducción y traductología. Introducción a la traductología.* Madrid: Cátedra.

Hutchins, W.J. 2001. Machine translation and human translation: in competition or in complementation? *International Journal of Translation,* 13: 5-20.

Hutchins, W.J. 1986. *Machine Translation. Past, Present and Future.* Chichester: Ellis Horwood Ltd.

Jääskeläinen, R. 2005. Translation studies: what are they? *Forskningsprosjekter. Workshops. Oslo.*

Jabak, O. 2008. Why is translation into the mother tongue more successful than into a second language? *Translation Directory.*

Jakobsen, A.L. 2006. Research Methods in Translation – Translog. In Sullivan, K.P.H. and E. Lindgren (eds) *Computer Keystroke Logging and Writing: Methods and Applications.* Oxford: Elsevier, 2-9.

Jakobson, R. 1966 (1959). On linguistic aspects of translation. In Brower (ed.) 1966: 232-239.

James, K. 2003. Cultural Implications for translation. *Translation Journal*, vol. 7, No. 1.

Kade, O. 1964. Ist alles übersetzbar? *Fremdsprachen*, 2: 84-99.

Kade, O. 1968. Zufall und Gesetzmässigkeit in der Übersetzung. In *Fremdsprachen: Zeitschrift für Übersetzer, Dolmetscher un Sprach-kundige 3* (Leipzig, 1981): 70-90.

Katan, D. 1999. *Translating Cultures. An Introduction for Translators, Interpreters and Mediators.* Manchester: St. Jerome.

Kenny, D. 2009. Equivalence. In Baker, M. and G. Saldanha (eds.) *Routledge Encyclopedia of Translation Studies.* London and New York: Routledge, 96-99.

Krings, H.P. 1986. Translation problems and translation strategies of advanced German learners of French. In House, J. and S. Blum-Kulka (eds.) *Interlingual and intercultural communication.* Tubingen: Gunter Narr, 263-276.

Ku, M. 2006. *La traducción de los elementos lingüísticos culturales (chino-español). Estudio de Sueño en las Estancias Rojas.* Tesis Doctoral. Bellaterra: Universitat Autònoma de Barcelona.

Kumar, B. 2008. Problems of translation. In Ray, M.K. (ed.) *Studies in Translation.* New Delhi: Atlantic Publishers and Distributors, Ltd., 45-65.

Kussmaul, P. 1995. *Training the Translator.* John Benjamins Publishing Co.

Kutz, W. 1983. La equivalencia cero (español-alemán) y rasgos esenciales de su superación translatoria. *Linguistische Arbeitsberichte. Theoretische und angewandte Sprachwissenschaft*, 40: 89-98.

Lambert, J. 1991. Shifts, Oppositions and Goals in Translation Studies: Towards a Genealogy of Concepts. In van Leuven-Zwart, K and T. Naaijkens (eds)

Translation Studies: The State of the Art. Amsterdam & Atlanta GA: Rodopi, 25-37.

Lázaro Carreter, F. 1974. *Diccionario de términos filológicos.* Madrid: Gredos.

Lederer, M. 1994. *La traduction aujourd'hui.* Paris: Hachette.

Leonardi, V. 2000. Equivalence in Translation: Between Myth and Reality. *Translation Journal*, vol. 4, No. 4.

Lewandowski, T. 1982. *Diccionario de Lingüística.* Madrid: Cátedra. (Original: *Linguistisches Wörterbuch.* Heildelberg: Quelle und Meyer).

López Guix, J.G. and J. Minett Wilkinson. 1999. *Manual de Traducción inglés / Castellano.* Barcelona: Editorial Gedisa.

Lorenzo, E. 1981. Utrum lingua an loquentes? (Sobre las presuntas dolencias y carencias de nuestro idioma). *Discurso de ingreso en la RAE. Publicaciones de la RAE.*

Lörscher, W. 1991. *Translation Performance, Translation Process, and Translation Strategies. A Psycholinguistic Investigation.* Tübingen: Gunter Narr.

Malmkjær, K. 2004. *Translation in Undergraduate Degree Programmes.* Amsterdam/Philadelphia: John Benjamins.

Malmkjaer, K. 2005. *Linguistics and the Language of translation.* Edinburgh: Edinburgh University Press.

Malmkjaer, K. 2011. Linguistic approaches to translation. In Malmkjaer, K. and K. Windle (eds.) *The Oxford Handbook of Translation Studies.* Oxford: Oxford University Press.

Malone, J.L. 1988. *The Science of Linguistics in the Art of Translation: Some tools from linguistics for the analysis and practice of translation.* Albany: State University of New York Press.

Marco Borillo, J. 2004. Les tècniques de traducció (dels referents culturals): retorn per a quedar-nos-hi. *Quaderns. Revista de traducció,* 11: 129-149.

Mayoral Asensio, R. 1994. La explicitación de la información en la traducción intercultural. In Hurtado Albir, A. (ed.) 1994: 73-96.

Mobaraki, M. and S. Aminzadeh. 2012. A study on different translation evaluation strategies to introduce an eclectic method. *International Journal of English Linguistics,* 2: 63-70.

Molina, L. 2001. *Análisis descriptivo de la traducción de los culturemas árabe-español.* Tesis Doctoral. Universitat Autònoma de Barcelona.

Molina, L. and A. Hurtado Albir. 2002. Translation Techniques Revisited: A Dynamic and Functionalist Approach. *Meta, XLVII,* 4: 498-512.

Moliner, M. 1998. *Diccionario de uso del español.* Madrid: Gredos.

Mott, B.L. 2011. *Semantics and Translation for Spanish Learners of English.* Barcelona: Universitat de Barcelona.

Mur Dueñas, M.P. 2003. Translating culture-specific references into Spanish: The Best a Man can Get. *Trans* 7: 71-84.

Neubert, A and G.M. Shreve. 1992. *Translation as Text.* Kent: Kent State Univ. Press.

Newmark, P. 1969. Some notes on translation and translators. *Incorporated Linguist, 8/4*: 79–85.

Newmark, P. 1988. *A Textbook of Translation.* London/New York: Prentice Hall.

Newmark, P. 1991. *About Translation.* Clevendon: Multilingual Matters.

Newmark, P. 1995. *A Textbook of Translation.* Library of Congress Cataloging-in-Publication Data.

Nida, E. 1975. *Componential Analysis of Meaning. An Introduction to Semantic Structures*. The Hague: Mouton.

Nida, E. y C.R. Taber. 1982 (1969). *The Theory and Practice of Translation*. Leiden: Brill [French edition: *La traduction: théorie et méthode*, 1971].

Nord, C. 1991. *Text Analysis in Translation. Theory, Methodology, and Didactic Applications of a Model for Translation-Oriented Text Analysis.* Amsterdam/Atlanta GA: Rodopi.

Nord, C. 1995. Text-Functions in Translation. *Target*, 7:2, 261-284.

Nord, C. 1997. A functional typology of translations. In Trosborg, A. (ed): *Text Typology and Translation*. Amsterdam: John Benjamins: 43-66.

Nord, C. 2001. *Translating as a Purposeful Activity: Functionalist Approaches Explained*. Manchester: St. Jerome.

Nord, C. 2006. Translating for Communicative Purposes across Culture Boundaries. *Journal of Translation Studies,* 9: 43-60.

Ordudari, M. 2008. Good Translation: Art, Craft, or Science? *Translation Journal* 12/1.

Ortega y Gasset, J. 1961 (1937). Miseria y esplendor de la traducción. In *Obras Completas V* (Madrid: Revista de Occidente): 433-452.

PACTE. 2003. Building a Translation Competence Model. In Alves, F. (ed.). *Triangulating Translation: Perspectives in Process Oriented Research.* Amsterdam: John Benjamins, 43-66.

Rabadán, R. 1991. *Equivalencia y traducción: Problemática de la equivalencia translémica inglés-español*. León: Universidad de León.

Real Academia Española. 2001. *DRAE: Diccionario de la Lengua Española*. Madrid: Espasa-Calpe.

Reiss, K. 1976. *Texttyp und Übersetzungsmethode. Der operative Text*. Kronberg TS: Scriptor Verlag.

Reiss, K. and H.J. Vermeer. 1984. *Grundlagen einer allgemeinen Translations-theorie.* Tübingen: Niemeyer.

Roberts, R.P. 1995. Towards a typology of translations. *Hieronymus,* 1: 69-78.

Rothe-Neves, R 2007. Notes on the concept of "translator's competence". *Quaderns. Revista de traducció*, 14: 125-138.

Santoyo, J.C. 1987. *Teoría y crítica de la traducción: Antología*. Bellaterrra: Universidad Autónoma de Barcelona.

Santoyo, J.C. 1994. Traducción de cultura, traducción de civilización. In Hurtado Albir, A. (ed.) 1994: 141-152.

Sapir, E. 1929. The Status of Linguistics as a Science. *Language,* 5: 209.

Schaffner, C. 1998. Action (Theory of Translational action). In Baker, M. (ed.) *Routledge Encyclopedia of Translation Studies*. London: Routledge, 3-5.

Shuttleworth, M. and M. Cowie. 1997. *Dictionary of Translation Studies*. Manchester: St. Jerome.

Snell-Hornby, M. 1988. *Translation Studies. An Integrated Approach*. Amsterdam: John Benjamins.

Snell-Hornby, M. 1991. Translation Studies - Art, Science or Utopia?. In van Leuven-Zwart, K. and T. Naaijkens (eds) *Translation Studies: The State of the Art.* Amsterdam & Atlanta GA: Rodopi, 13-23.

Snell-Hornby, M. 2006. *The Turns of Translation Studies: New Paradigms Or Shifting Viewpoints?* Amsterdam: John Brnjamins.

Torre, E. 1994. *Teoría de la traducción literaria*. Madrid: Síntesis.

Toury, G. 1980. *In Search of a Theory of Translation*. Tel Aviv: The Porter Institute for Poetics and Semiotics.

Toury, G. 1991. What are Descriptive Studies into Translation Likely to Yield apart from Isolated Descriptions?. In van Leuven-Zwart, K. and T. Naaijkens (eds.) *Translation Studies: The State of the Art*. Amsterdam & Atlanta GA: Rodopi, 179-192.

Toury, G. 1995. *Descriptive Translation Studies and Beyond*. Amsterdam/ Philadelphia: John Benjamins.

Ulitkin, I. 2011. Computer-assisted Translation Tools: A brief review. *Translation Journal*, Volume 15, No. 1.

Vázquez Ayora, G. 1977. *Introducción a la traductología*. Washington, D.C.: Georgetown University Press.

Vinay, J.P. and J. Darbelnet. 1977 (1958). *Stylistique comparée du français et de l'anglais*. París: Didier.

Vlakhov, S. and S. Florin. 1970. Neperovodimoe v perevode. *Realii, in Masterstvo perevoda, n. 6, 1969, Moskvà, Sovetskij pisatel*: 432-456.

Whorf, B. 1956. *Language, Thought and Reality*. Cambridge, Mass.: The M.I.T. Press.

Williams, M. 2009. Translation Quality Asessdment. *Mutatis Mutandis*, 2: 3-23.

Wilpert, G. von 1979. *Sachwörterbuch der Literatur*. Stuttgart: Kröner.

Wilss, W. 1982. *The Science of Translation. Problems and Methods*. Tübingen: Gunter Narr.

Yifeng, S. 2012. (Un)translatability and cross-cultural readability. *Perspectives: Studies in Translatology*, 20(2): 231-247.